T H E
776
E V E N
STUPIDER
T H I N G S
EVER SAID

ALSO BY
ROSS AND
KATHRYN
PETRAS

The 776
Stupidest
Things Ever Said

THE 776 EVEN STUPIDER THINGS EVER SAID

ROSS AND KATHRYN PETRAS

HarperPerennial
A Division of HarperCollins Publishers

To Hugh Lovegren,
who loves stupid quotes,
and to George Petras, who inspires them

Library of Congress Cataloging-in-Publication Data

Petras, Ross.
    The 776 even stupider things ever said / Ross and Kathryn Petras.
    —1st ed.
        p.   cm.
    ISBN 0-06-095059-5
    1. Quotations, English. 2. Wit and humor.   I. Petras, Kathryn.
II. Title. III. Title: Seven hundred seventy-six even stupider things ever said.
PN6081.P448 1994   93-44804

    96 97 98 ❖/HC 10 9 8 7 6 5 4 3 2

ACKNOWLEDGMENTS

Thanks to everybody who helped make this book a reality, especially:
Kris Dahl, Dorothea Herrey, Susan Moldow and Nancy Peske for giving us the chance to be stupid the second time around; to Joseph Montebello and Mort Drucker for their magnificent visualization of stupidity; to Andre Barcinski, Paulo Cesar Martin and the staff of the Rio de Janeiro newspaper *Noticias Populares* for proof that stupidity exists in any language; to Mark S. Stewart and the folks at Philadelphia law firm Ballard Spahr Andrews & Ingersoll for recognizing the genius of partner Jim Coleman and to Jim Coleman for his unique flair for the quotable quote; to Susie James and James Dudgeon for supplying crucial last-minute information—and, of course, to all the others who contributed their favorite stupidities.

Great thoughts live on forever—why not dumb ones? With that great (or stupid) thought in mind, we compiled our second, better-than-ever *776 Even Stupider Things Ever Said*.

To paraphrase Jon Peters, producer of the megahit *Batman*, this isn't a sequel to our first collection, it's a second episode.

This one includes not-so-great thoughts from everyone from President Clinton to Voltaire, sports players and sportscasters, rock stars and bureaucrats—a cross-section of twisted, mangled, and garbled utterances from famous and not-so-famous people from around the globe.

In collecting the quotes for this book, we learned that saying something stupid isn't as straightforward as you'd think. Actually, there are different *ways* of saying something stupid. There's:

    • The Basic Stupid Misstatement—which occurs when your mouth is moving faster than your brain . . . and somehow the wrong word comes out at the wrong time. (Politicians and sportscasters are masters at this.)

    • The Classic Malaprop—which is, probably, the most memorable type of stupidity, when you garble clichés, words, and syntax into a unique mix that, like a fine vintage wine, becomes a classic. (The geniuses here are Yogi Berra, Sam Goldwyn, Dan Quayle, and Sir Boyle Roche.)

• The Rambling Man (or Woman) Run-on—which is what you'd think it is—you start talking and you go on and on and on . . . usually without making much sense. (Ronald Reagan and Casey Stengel were true Rambling Men.)

• The Syntax Shuffle—which happens when you forget all those boring grammatical rules you were taught in school and instead slosh together all different sorts of verb tenses, adverbs, pronouns, and connectors into a logic-defying mash. (A favorite of George Bush and Dwight Eisenhower.)

• The Terror Translations—which happens when you hire the wrong translator to transform your wonderful thoughts into another language. (Famous examples include JFK's "I am a jelly donut" speech and Jimmy Carter's "I lust for the Poles" speech.)

• Doublespeak—an old favorite of the Pentagon, press secretaries, bureaucrats, academics, PR types, and anyone else who wants to say as little as possible in as many words as possible.

• The Outrageous Stupidity—often the most frightening kind of stupid statement, which happens when people say something clearly out of bounds of normal decency, ethics, or thought. It leaves you wondering: Is that what they *really* think?

• The Old-Fashioned Spoonerism—named for the Reverend William Spooner of England, who had a habit of mixing up the first letters or syllables of different words and wound up with some bizarre results.

• The Truly Weird Typo—which, unlike most typically dull typographical errors, puts a new spin on an otherwise routine newspaper story.

• The Standard Just Plain Dumb Statement—which needs no explanation.

But, whatever the types of stupidity someone says, the end result is the same—they make you laugh . . . and that's why we've collected them for this book.

We'd like to hear from you. . . .

If you have a favorite stupidity that isn't in this book, send it in! We'd love to use it in our sequel—and we're always eager to see more of the best of the stupidest.

Send your stupid quotes to:

Ross & Kathryn Petras

c/o HarperCollins

10 E. 53rd Street

New York, NY 10022

(Please include a copy of your source, or the date, time and place you heard it—and let us know if you want to be credited in print for your contribution.)

On Ability:
> Not only is he ambidextrous, but he can throw with either hand.
> *Duffy Daugherty, former Michigan State coach turned sports analyst,*
> *providing on-air color commentary*

On Achievement:
> We shall reach greater and greater platitudes of achievement.
> *Richard J. Daley, mayor of Chicago*

On Activity:
> This scene has a lot of activity. It is busy like a bee dive.
> *Michael Curtiz, director, to film extras*

On Actors' Roles:

Cheer up, Freddy. You've got the best part in the picture. And you, Anna, you've got the best part too!

movie mogul Samuel Goldwyn to two actors in one of his films

On Actors, Sensitivity of:

Sure the body count in this movie bothers me, but what are you gonna do? It's what everybody likes. At least it's not an awful body count—it's a fun body count.

actress Bonnie Bedelia, star of Die Harder, *in a* Movies USA *interview*

On Advancement:

Our troops advanced today without losing a foot of ground.

British war communiqué

On Advantages:

It's a great advantage to be able to hurdle with both legs.

David Coleman, BBC sports commentator, known for his gaffes called "Colemanballs" in England, covering the 1992 Olympics on air

On Advertising Campaigns, Great Moments in:

Suzuki coffee: Your Last Impression.

Japanese advertisement

On Advice:

You've got to take the sour with the bitter.

> *movie mogul Samuel Goldwyn, reassuring director Billy Wilder after one of their films bombed*

On Aeronautics, Minor Problems in:

[The Air Force is pleased with the performance of the C-5A cargo plane, although] having the wings fall off at 8000 hours is a problem.

> *Major General Charles F. Kuyk, Jr.*

On Agendas, Hidden:

[The president of the National Association of State Fire Marshals] is available to comment on the critical need for deadly fires.

> *from a 1993 press release from the National Association of State Fire Marshals*

On Aging:

We all get heavier as we get older because there's a lot more information in our heads.

> *Vlade Divac, Los Angeles Lakers player*

On Agonizing Decisions:

They were torn between two fires.

> *Congressman John Dent*

On Agreeing:

If you don't disagree with me, how will I know I'm right?
movie mogul Samuel Goldwyn to author Sidney Kingsley

On Airlines:

AEROFLOT: Introducing wide boiled aircraft for your comfort. . . .
ad for the Soviet (Russian) airline Aeroflot

On Airports, Endangered:

Ag land is not sacred. It's a green area on a map. But an airport is a resource that needs to be protected.
Steve Dana, mayor of Snohomish, Washington, during a land-annexation debate

On Aliens, What to Do with:

[The church] would be obliged to address the question of whether extraterrestrials might be brought within the fold and baptized.
Jesuit Father George Coyne, Vatican Observatory director, after the Vatican had begun working with NASA to locate extraterrestrials with a new telescope, on what to do if aliens were discovered

On Alphabetizing:

Line up alphabetically by height.
Casey Stengel, baseball great

On the AMA, Possible Hidden Agenda of:

Many groups in America face health risks: children, adolescents, the elderly, the homeless, women. The AMA is committed to speaking out on their behalf . . . establishing programs and policies that protect and defeat their rights to a long and healthy life.

from an American Medical Association letter sent to resident doctors

On Ambassadors (Would-Be), Country Analyses by:

I think they are a people who are friendly and unfriendly.

Maxwell Gluck, Eisenhower nominee to be ambassador to Ceylon, before a Senate hearing. He was not confirmed.

On Ambassadors, Qualifications for Becoming:

"English (fluent)"

Listed as his language proficiency by U.S. Ambassador to Australia, Melvin Sembler, on his résumé

On Ambassadors, Qualifications for Becoming:

I am sure I will feel at home in the Bahamas. I've been involved in gambling in the Bahamas. I've been involved in gambling in Nevada and I've been involved in banking.

Chic Hecht, former senator from Nevada, while testifying for an appointment to be ambassador to the Bahamas. He was appointed.

On Anatomy:

This coach is crazy. He can't ask me to run like this. He must think I have two lungs.

> *player from the Brazilian soccer team Rio Claro, complaining to a TV reporter; as collected by Paulo Cesar Martin and the staff of the newspaper* Noticias Populares

On Anglo-American Friendship, the British View:

It underscores our intention to play an even more vigorous role on behalf of the organisations, and individuals, who compromise our membership. . . .

> *from a letter by Colin Draper, president of the British-American Chamber of Commerce*

On Answering Phones:

I'm out, but call me back in an hour.

> *Michael Curtiz, film director, to a phone caller*

On Answers, Multiplying:

I am providing you with a copulation of answers to several questions raised. . . .

> *letter from Marion Barry, Jr., mayor of Washington, D.C.*

On Apostles, High Cost of Filming:

Twelve? So who needs *twelve*? Couldn't we make do with *six*?

> *Lew Grade, British producer and media tycoon, when told by Franco*

Zeffirelli, director of the film Jesus of Nazareth, *that one of the reasons the cost of the film was so high was that there had to be twelve apostles*

On the Apostles, Twelve:

Samuel Goldwyn: Why only twelve?

Employee: That's the original number.

Goldwyn: Well, go out and get thousands.

    attributed to movie mogul Samuel Goldwyn, when filming The Last Supper

On Apprehension:

Reporter: Were you apprehensive in the twelfth inning?

Yogi Berra: No, but I was scared

On Arms, Sore:

I wouldn't say that Joe has a sore arm, per se, but his arm is kind of sore.

    Weeb Ewbank, New York Jets coach, answering questions on Joe Namath's absence from a practice

On Artists, Living:

He [Francis Bacon] was probably our greatest living painter—until he died.

    LBC (British television) news presenter

On Artists, Starving:

I'm limited to the income I can have as an artist. I can make maybe several million a year if I'm extremely successful, but I could never come into the $100 million a year range, the half billion a year range. . . .

artist Jeff Koons, during a public television interview

On Artistic Sensibility:

What good is the moon if you can't buy it or sell it?

Ivan Boesky, Wall Street trader, eventually convicted of insider trading

On Asses, Cecil B. DeMille Movies and:

The jawbone of an ass! Never! This is a DeMille picture and we've got to use the *whole* ass!

assistant to director Cecil B. DeMille, when filming Samson and Delilah *and discussing the scene in which Samson slays the Philistines with the jawbone of an ass*

On Assessments, Logical:

Our strength is that we don't have any weaknesses. Our weakness is that we don't have any real strengths.

Frank Broyles, University of Arkansas football coach, on the team's prospects

On Athletes, Great:

Michael Jordan, one of the world's greatest defenders—if not one of the best. . . .

> *David Coleman, British sportscaster, known for his on-air gaffes called "Colemanballs" in England*

On Autobiographies:

I don't think anybody should write his autobiography until after he's dead.

> *movie mogul Samuel Goldwyn*

On Babar the Children's Elephant, Agenda of:

[Babar] extols the virtues of a European middle-class life-style and disparages the animals and people who have remained in the jungle.

Patricia Ramsey, director of the Gorse Child Studies Center, Massachusetts

On Babies, the Joy of:

Every newborn baby is a little savage.

Daryl Gates, former LAPD chief

On Baby Boomers, Fantasies of.

Every woman I know is having sex dreams about Bill Clinton.

staffer at The Boomer Report, *a monthly newsletter, as quoted in the* National Review, *February 1, 1993*

On Bachelor Life:

A bachelor's life is no life for a single man.

movie mogul Samuel Goldwyn

On Bad Calls:

I don't need bodyguards.

Jimmy Hoffa, labor leader who was later missing and presumed murdered, in a December 1975 Playboy *interview*

On Bad Film Lines:

In a house like this you wouldn't want to be alone unless there were plenty of people around.

woman in You'll Find Out, *1940s thriller*

On Bali, Reasons to Visit:

If we are lucky we will see duck boys bringing their ducks home, men massaging their cocks on the road, cow boys taking grass. Yes it is a wonderful experience. Don't miss it during your visit to the island of the gods, Bali.

Tunas Indonesia Tours & Travel brochure

On Bands, Different:
Now coming onto the field to entertain the fans is the Air Force Academy Drug and Bugle Corps.

Larry King, TV personality, on air during a Miami Dolphins–Baltimore Colts game

On Baseball Managing, Casey Stengel Explaining:
That feller runs splendid but he needs help at the plate, which coming from the country chasing rabbits all winter give him strong legs, although he broke one falling out of a tree, which shows you can't tell, and when a curve ball comes he waves at it and if pitchers don't throw curves you have no pitching staff, so how is a manager going to know whether to tell boys to fall out of trees and break legs so he can run fast even if he can't hit a curve ball?

Casey Stengel, baseball great

On Baseball Managing, Yogi Berra Explaining:
The other teams could make trouble for us if they win.

Yogi Berra, then Yankee manager

On Bases, Character of:
The players returned to their respectable bases.

Dizzy Dean, baseball great, on air

On the Basics:

We've been working on the basics because, basically, we've been having trouble with the basics.

Bob Ojeda, L.A. Dodgers pitcher

On Basketball:

Ball handling and dribbling are my strongest weaknesses.

David Thompson, Denver Nuggets player

On Bathhouse Behavior, Proper:

Foreigners are requested not to pull cock in Japanese bath.

sign in a Japanese ski resort lodge

On Battle Orders, Helpful:

Elevate them guns a little lower!

President Andrew Jackson, at the battle of Mobile, Alabama, in 1815

On Beating, Correct Forms of:

We are the best police department in the world, but we are not perfect. Rodney King should never have been hit fifty-six times, yet many of the blows which struck him were correctly placed so as not to cause serious injury, exactly as we teach in the Academy.

Daryl F. Gates, former Los Angeles police chief, in his book Chief: My Life in the LAPD

On Beethoven, Hobbies of:

Beethoven had ten children and practiced on a spinster in the attic.
famous typo from the old Philadelphia Bulletin

On Beginnings:

You fought the good fight. You were in it right up to the beginning.
Bruce Babbitt, Secretary of the Interior

On Beginnings:

Enos Cabell started out here with the Astros. And before that he was with the Orioles.
Jerry Coleman, San Diego Padres announcer

On Beginnings:

Our first move will be to decide what our first move will be.
Wellington Mara, New York Giants president, explaining what they intended to do after firing their head coach and accepting the resignation of the director of operations

On Beginnings:

I concluded from the beginning that this would be the end; and I am right, for it is not half over yet.
Sir Boyle Roche, eighteenth century member of Parliament from Tralee, famed for his word mangling

On Beheading Drug Dealers:

Morally, there's no problem with that at all. I used to teach ethics—trust me.

Drug Czar William Bennett

On Bellwethers, Following:

I just don't happen to belong to that branch of the sheep family that will follow a bellwether over a precipice.

Representative John Ashbrook (R-Ohio)

On Bills, Congressional:

If every man insists on knowing what he's voting for before he votes, we're not going to get a bill reported before Monday.

Senator Russell B. Long (D-Louisiana)

On Blessings, Self-Referential:

God Bless the Holy Trinity

placard in a Dublin parade

On Bondage:

Republicans understand the importance of bondage between a mother and child.

Vice President Dan Quayle

On Bonsais, Militaristic:

Under the overall supervision of Hirohito's uncle, Prince Asaka, Hirohito's bonsai-shouting imperial army embarked on six weeks of "wholesale atrocities and barbarism."

from an ad placed in the New York Times. *Bonsai are miniature trees.*

On Boogers, Waving:

We'll run it up the flagpole and see who salutes that booger.

Gib Lewis, speaker of the Texas House

On Book Reviews, Great:

. . . She holds the words in her hands like voluptuous breasts, plump and firm. She strokes, kisses, weighs and admires them until they shine. . . . Words roll around in her mouth like blue grapes before the teeth pierce them and the juice explodes onto the reader's palate.

Susan Mitchell, writing about author Jeanette Winterson in the Adelaide (Australia) Review

On Books, Must-Read:

The Glove in Law, in Government Administration, in Custom, and in Popular Belief, by Dr. Berent Schwinekoper

title of German book, circa 1940, published by Berlin publishing house Junker und Dunnhaupt

On Boxing:

I don't believe in stopping fights. Even if a guy is getting too much of a beating. You shouldn't be prolonging a guy's career. If he's done, let him be done. It's like a mercy killing.

Jake La Motta, boxer

On Boxing Bach:

Journalist: What is your opinion of Bach?
Chalky Wright (a fighter who claimed to be a classical music fan): A very clever boy. He can't miss.

On Boys, Relationships with Other Species:

A rat is a pig is a dog is a boy.

Ingrid Newkirk, animal rights activist, as quoted in the Seattle Post-Intelligencer

On Bravery:

Venison and Butcher—they were both as brave as two peas in a pod.

John Sillett, Central TV

On the Brooklyn Dodgers, Where They Were:

They brought me up to the Brooklyn Dodgers, which at that time was in Brooklyn.

Casey Stengel, baseball great

On Brotherly Love:

Erected in the memory of
John Phillips
Accidentally shot
As a mark of affection by his brother.

inscription on a gravestone

On Brothers, Presidential:

It's been a long time since either one of us has gone out of each other's way to contact the other.

Roger Clinton, brother of President Bill Clinton, explaining his relationship with Hillary Clinton

On Call to Arms, Stirring:

On questions of war and peace there is a societal imperative for caution, but it must be understood that ambivalence is not synonymous with statesmanship and that anxietyship is no substitute for leadership.

> *Representative Jim Leach (R-Iowa) during the congressional debate about sending troops to the Persian Gulf, as quoted in the Congressional Record (Note—Leach didn't serve in Vietnam; he got a student deferment, then a medical deferment)*

On Campaign Speeches, Great Moments in:

We have been pushing the idea that George Bush is going to make matters much, much, worse.

> *Vice President Dan Quayle, campaigning for Bush in the 1992 election*

On Campaign Speeches, Great Moments in:

My heart is as black as yours. . . .

> *Mario Procaccino, Democratic candidate for New York mayor in 1969, to an African American audience*

On Candidates, Why Not to Vote for:

Wennlund has an obscure, undistinguished record, and he's a poor dresser, too.

> *Ray Hanania, candidate for Illinois state representative, talking about incumbent Larry Wennlund*

On Capitalism, Great Thoughts About:

The private enterprise system indicates that some people have higher incomes than others.

> *Jerry Brown, then governor of California*

On Cars, Gassy:

In speed record attempts, the cyclist pedals just a few meters behind a car that breaks wind for the rider.

> *item in* South China Morning Post, *about a Dutch cyclist*

On Cars, Great Names for:

Utopian Turtletop

> *name for a new Ford car thought up by Marianne Moore, famous American poet. Henry Ford had commmissioned her to come up with the name; after hearing her idea, he decided against it and went with another name—the Edsel*

On Casting:

Maybe I can find some major league suspects.

> *Johnny Logan, ex-Milwaukee Braves shortstop, while working as a casting adviser on a film*

On Casting Calls, Bad:

Ears too big.

> *anonymous Hollywood casting director after Clark Gable's first screen test*

On Casting Calls, Bad:

You have a chip on your tooth, your Adam's Apple sticks out too far and you talk too slow.

> *a Universal Pictures executive to Clint Eastwood*

On Casting Calls, Bad:

Can't act. Can't sing. Balding. Can dance a little.

> *MGM exec about Fred Astaire's screen test*

On Casting Calls (the Flip Side), Bad:

Gone with the Wind is going to be the biggest flop in Hollywood history. I'm just glad it'll be Clark Gable who's falling flat on his face and not Gary Cooper.

> *Gary Cooper, after he turned down the role of Rhett Butler*

On Castration, Motivational:

Jackie Sherrill apologized Tuesday for allowing the castration of a bull in front of his Mississippi State football team. . . . The bull was castrated in front of the team on a practice field. . . . Later Sherrill said he allowed the procedure because it was educational and motivational.

> *an item from the Associated Press news wire*

On Catch-22s:

If the Executive Committee had been all white, it would have been merely a traditional racist act, typical of the old "last hired, first fired" format. If it had been carried out by an all-black Executive Committee, as at Tuskegee or Fisk, it would have been elitist. That the purge was executed by an integrated committee, and liberal at that, makes it neoracist: that is fusing together both the question of class and race.

> *Activist Finely Campbell, on the reasons why the liberal University of Wisconsin failed to grant him tenure*

On Censorship:

Omit "You get all the dirt off the tail of your shirt." Substitute "You get all the dirt off the front of your shirt." . . . Omit the song "Plastic Mac Man" and substitute "Oh you dirty young devil, how dare you presume to wet the bed when the po's in the room. I'll wallop your bum with a dirty great broom when I get up in the morning."

> *Office of the Lord Chamberlain, British theater censor until 1968, as quoted in* Tynan Right and Life, *by K. Tynan*

On Censorship:

. . . the film is apparently meaningless, but if it has any meaning it is doubtless objectionable.

> *British Board of Film Censors, on Jean Cocteau's* The Seashell and the Clergyman

On Censorship, Great Moments in:

American journalist in Japan, just prior to World War II, in a letter:
Don't know if this will ever arrive because the Japanese censor may open it.

Japanese post office note to the journalist, sent a few days later:
The statement in your letter is not correct. We do not open letters.

On Certainty, Absolute:

If there's one thing we're certain of, it's our certitudes.

> *White House official to a* Wall Street Journal *reporter, explaining that then-President Ronald Reagan would be seeking a second term*

On Challenges:

. . . We're not afraid of challenges. It's like I always say: if you want to go out in the rain, be prepared to get burned.

> *soccer player from Brazilian team Rio Claro, to a TV reporter, as collected by Paulo Cesar Martin and the staff of the* Noticias Populares *newspaper*

On Change, Understanding:

Changing someone's life is not the best, is not wanting to change the other life. It is being who you are that changes another's life. Do you understand?

> *Juliette Binoche, actress in films such as* Damage, *in a 1992 interview*

On Charisma:

Player: One of our players has real charisma.
University of Oklahoma coach: What? Will he be okay by Saturday?

On Charity:

Filipinos want beauty. I have to look beautiful so that the poor Filipinos will have a star to look at from their slums.

> *Imelda Marcos, former Philippine first lady*

On Cheerleaders:

Tell me. These women—are they wayward?

> *Viktor Thkhonov, Russian hockey team coach, watching the cheerleaders at a Minnesota–Dallas football game*

On Chemical Weapons, Not-so-Bad:

Strictly as a weapon of war, chemicals are by no means the most inhumane weapons we have. Artillery fire, for example, spreads the victim's body all over the landscape.

> *Admiral William J. Crowe, Jr., in an interview with the Los Angeles* Times

On Childhood, Long:

Mr. Englund has been a childhood friend of mine for some 30 to 35 years. . . .

> *Hoboken, New Jersey, campaign manager for the Richard Englund mayoral campaign*

On Childhood, Longer:

We have been boyhood friends all of our lives.

> *Chicago Mayor Richard Daley during the Chicago Seven trial*

On Children, Congressional Compassion for:

We were able to slow down and dilute child care.

> *Senator Bob Dole (R-Kansas) actually speaking of a child-care bill*

On China, a Fun Place to Visit:

Don't squat when waiting for a bus or a person. Don't spit in public. Don't point at people with your fingers. Don't make noise. Don't laugh loudly. Don't yell or call to people from a distance. Don't pick your teeth, pick your nose, blow your nose, pick at your ears, rub your eyes, or rub dirt off your skin. Don't scratch, take off your shoes, burp, stretch or hum.

Chinese government-issued list of travelers' tips

On Chiropractics, War-Stopping Ability of:

Had ex-Kaiser Wilhelm received chiropractic adjustments for whatever abnormal conditions from which he was suffering, the World War would have been averted.

Charles B. Loftin, vice president of the San Antonio College of Chiropractors in an Associated Press item

On Civil Rights, Great Strides Made in:

That's all very well, but two blacks don't make a white.

Michael Barratt, broadcaster and author, when interviewing two arguing black Rhodesian politicians—and meaning to say, "Two wrongs don't make a right"

On Civil Rights, Great Strides Made in:

Nelson Rockefeller, while watching African American Congressman Ed Brooke greeting the Liberian president:

Ed Brooke is a one-man receiving committee.

Carl Albert, speaker of the House:

Yeah, he'd be a slave if he were over there.

> *(This interchange was accidentally broadcast over an open mike)*

On Civil Rights, Great Strides Made in:

Oh, come on now—he's talking about blacks. Let's call a spade a spade.

> *Gerald Harper, speaking about Winston Churchill*

On Civil Rights, Great Strides Made in:

We haven't had any problem here about race. We just don't go for letting the colored ones in.

> *Rainbow Girls leader in Branford, Connecticut, commenting in the* New Haven Register *about the fact that blacks were not allowed to become Rainbow Girls*

On Civil Servants, Very Dedicated:

Hal was an effective commissioner right up to the end and beyond.

> *Carl Hansen, Cook County, Illinois, commissioner, on a recently deceased colleague*

On Clarity, Congressional:

Some action of a definite responsive nature probably needs to be taken if it's absolutely clear, but it isn't, at least in the public sphere, clear that the evidence is overwhelming or without any ambiguity.

> *Thomas Foley, House Speaker (D-Wash.), on the TV program "Face the Nation," commenting on reports that the Iraqi government had planned to assassinate President George Bush*

On Clichés:

Let's have some new clichés.

> *movie mogul Samuel Goldwyn*

On Clichés:

Most of my clichés aren't original.

> *Chuck Knox, Los Angeles Rams coach*

On Clichés, Simian Political:

To use a cliché, we orangutanged the front office. We orangutang the hospitals and bring them into a bill. . . . Let's not kid ourselves. We're orangutanged. That's what we are, brought right in.

> *Charles F. Sylvia, Massachusetts state representative, on the health-care bill*

On Clichés, Texan:

We don't want to skim the cream off the crop here.

> *Gib Lewis, Speaker of the Texas House*

On Close Calls:

Well, that was a cliff-dweller.
Wes Westrum, Mets coach, on a very close game

On Clothing, Revealing:

It's a hot night at the Garden, folks, and at ringside I see several ladies in gownless evening straps.
Jimmy Powers, radio sportscaster

On Coats, Fur:

Fur coats made for ladies from their own skin.
sign at a Swedish furrier, from an exhibit sponsored by the European Community's translation service

On Coats, Unusual:

It's got lots of installation.
Mike Smith, Cincinnati Reds relief pitcher, extolling the virtues of his new coat

On Coffee, Reasons for Glowing:

They do not normally make coffee from this [radioactive] water, but yesterday one of the employees felt perhaps demineralized water makes better coffee than tap water. That's how it got utilized.
Donald C. Cook, nuclear power plant official, explaining how radioactive water from the plant was used to make coffee

On Colors, Corporate:

It's a very blue-green, almost blue, but it would still be classified in our terms as green. When we were selling this color—because we had not had green in the lineup for so long—to get people comfortable with it we did not call it green, we called it blue.

> *Bonnie Cunningham, design manager for colors for Ford, on the Cougar's "pastel steel blue frost," as quoted in the* Miami Herald

On Colors, Loud:

Hark! I hear a white horse coming!

> *from the old* Lone Ranger *radio program*

On Colors, Military:

Their uniforms were all different, chiefly green.

> *Sir Boyle Roche, eighteenth century member of Parliament from Tralee, famed for his word mangling*

On Coming Clean:

I have nothing else to say. We—we did—if—the—the—I—I—the stories are just as they have been said.

> *President Bill Clinton, when asked if the stories about his extramarital affairs while he was Governor of Arkansas were true*

On Commissions, Macho Chicago:

[I propose to create a] Commission on Erections and Mounting.

> *Richard M. Daley, Jr., Mayor of Chicago, proposing to honor the late Everett Dirksen with a statue, and to create a commission to look into the matter*

On Communism, Great Claims of:

We are not without accomplishment. We have managed to distribute poverty equally.

Nguyen Co Thach, foreign minister of Vietnam

On Compliments:

Darling, you stink so beautiful.

Michael Curtiz, film director, to a perfumed actress

On Compliments:

What a picture! It will be a feather in your eye!

Harry Rapf, film director

On Computers, Uterine:

Aphra Benn was the first Englishwoman to make her living "by her pen," as we used to say. Now nobody makes her—or his—living by the phallic and virile pen. Linguistic and cultural structures no longer combine in exhibiting the exciting transgression, the impudent androgyny, of the man-woman who picks up her pen to write, for the she-writer, like the he-writer, will feed symbols through the word-processor, a brooding matrix-box far more uterine than penile.

Margaret Anne Doody, in the London Review of Books

On Conclusions, Unassailable:

As I've said before and I said yesterday, this is one of the key questions which will be decided or not decided at Edinburgh.

Douglas Hurd, member of Parliament

On Congress, Great Laws Made by:

The Public Printer shall not publish in the *Congressional Record* the full report or print of any committee or subcommittee when the report or print has been previously printed. This rule shall not be construed to apply to conference reports. However, inasmuch as House of Representatives Rule XXVII, Section 912, provides that conference reports be printed in the daily edition of the *Congressional Record,* they shall not be printed therein a second time.

> *Section 9, "Laws and Rules of the* Congressional Record,*" as amended, circa 1976*

On Congress, Problems with:

The Congress is just full of Germans and Italians. They should be taken out of office and prosecuted.

> *Robert Roosevelt, senatorial candidate from Maryland*

On Congressional Open-Mindedness:

Nothing any witness could say would change my mind on the subject at all.

> *Senator Key Pittman, chairman of the Senate Foreign Relations Committee in the 1930s*

On Congressional Wisdom:

When you get married you might expect you're going to get a little sex.

> *Senator Jeremiah Denton on why rape legislation for victims within the marriage was not a good idea*

On Congressional Wisdom:

Those who survived the San Francisco earthquake said, "Thank God, I'm still alive." But, of course, those who died, their lives will never be the same again.

Representative Barbara Boxer (D-California)

On Congressional Wisdom:

I've tried everything else to convince you. Now I'm going to be sensible.

unnamed congressman during debate

On Conscientious Objector Status, Reasons for Not Attaining:

As a doctor, Major Ladner is involved in killing forms of life that also can be seen as having a path to live, such as viral and bacteriological entities.

Conscientious Objector Review Board of the U.S. Army, turning down an application for the CO discharge of Major Monte Ladner, a U.S. Army doctor who served during the Gulf War

On Consumers, FTC Protection of:

Imperfect products should be available because consumers have different preferences for defect avoidance.

James Miller, Federal Trade Commission chairman

On Contacts:

Traffic cop: Your driver's license says you wear glasses. Why aren't you wearing them?

Phil Linz, ballplayer: I got contacts.

Traffic cop: I don't care who you know, you still have to wear glasses when you drive.

On Contortions:

This isn't a man who is leaving with his head between his legs.

Vice President Dan Quayle, during a television interview, when asked about then Chief of Staff John Sununu's resignation

On Convictions, Political:

I believe in unions and I believe in non-unions.

President George Bush

On Convictions, Political:

[It] obviously puts a serious crimp in my political future.

Representative Andrew J. Hinshaw, on his conviction for two counts of felony bribery

On the Correctional System, Wisdom of:

We're just mystified as to why he [an inmate] did what he did [killed a kitchen worker]. He never gave a clue that he was this type of violent person. Based on his record, he has had some alcohol offenses, but no other offenses of this nature—aside from the beating death of his wife.

Andy Bowen, Georgia prison spokesman

On Corrections by the Independent Egyptian Press:

A confusion happened and a mistake was made. I attributed these comments to the President, but in fact they came in the analysis, explanation and information which the editors put before the President, quoting American newspapers and media.

> *Mahfouz al Ansari, Egyptian editor, after he quoted Egyptian President*
> *Mubarak a bit too accurately for Mubarak's taste*

On Corrections, Communist-Style:

In the article "Devote Every Effort to Running Successfully Socialist Research Institutes" (Sci. Sin. Vol XIX, No. 5), "the arch unrepentant capitalist-roader in the Party Teng Hsiao-ping" should read "Teng Hsiao-ping."

> *From the* Journal of the Chinese Academy of Sciences, *1977*

On Counting Words:

One word sums up probably the responsibility of any vice president. And that one word is "to be prepared."

> *Vice President Dan Quayle*

On Covering All Bases:

We're going to move left and right at the same time.

> *Jerry Brown, governor of California*

On Credit Cards, God and:

Sow a seed on your MasterCard, your Visa or your American Express, and then when you do, expect God to open the windows of heaven and pour you out a blessing.

Richard Roberts, televangelist

On Criminal Chiropractics:

The said board shall have the authority to revoke the license of any person practicing chiropractic in the State of Arkansas who has *not* been convicted in this state or elsewhere for the commission of any crime. . . .

Arkansas State law, section 11, act 485

On Critics:

Don't pay any attention to the critics—don't even ignore them.

movie mogul Samuel Goldwyn

On Cubes:

And what shape, then, is the Rubik's Cube?

Peter Sissons, BBC

On Cubs Fans, Comforting Thoughts for:

This is no longer a slum neighborhood. I haven't heard of a Cubs fan being shot in a long time.

resident of the Wrigley Field area

On Culture and Explosives:

More cultured people may not want to be hired because of the danger here. A less educated person has more courage to work with dangerous substances.

> *Arildo Resende, explosives plant manager in Cabo, Brazil*

On Customer Service; Frightening:

Order your summers suit. Because is big rush we will execute customers in strict rotation.

> *sign in a Rhodes tailor shop*

On Customs, Declaration Forms:

Objects must be declared. If there isn't any object mark "X" only at the quantity "Yes" column and if there are any objects, cross out letter "No" and at the same row write exact amount of weight of these objects in words or in figures.

> *customs form, Socialist Republic of Vietnam, Question 10, which also warns sternly against "giving false declaration or having the action of tricking." From* Return to Saigon, *Kitty Kelly, 1992*

SPECIAL SECTION:
The Stupidest Brand Names

As the line by Shakespeare goes, A rose by any other name would smell as sweet.

Wrong.

Sounds great, but it just doesn't work that way. Picture this: It's a hot day. You're thirsty. So you go to the refrigerator and grab an ice-cold . . .

Mucos.

That's the name of a Japanese soft drink. And it doesn't quite conjure up the right image—which is what brand names are supposed to do, after all.

Any product—a car, a candy bar, a colonoscope—needs a snappy name to make it stand out from the crowd. Which is why brand names were invented. We don't go shopping for a generic car, we shop for a Thunderbird.

But for all the marketing whizzes and advertising geniuses, somehow something goes wrong and a product gets a name like, well, Mucos.

This kind of unfortunate nomenclature is all the more common when corporations try to sell their wares globally. Sometimes they don't do their homework. Or they get the wrong translator.

Which is why such monumental blunders occur, like translating Coca-Cola into "Bite the Wax Tadpole" for the Chinese market. Not many Chinese would jump at the chance at buying a bottle of sparkling "Bite the Wax Tadpole." And Chevrolet was ready to sell the "It Doesn't Go" car in Latin America. That's what Spanish speakers read when they saw the Chevy "Nova."

In the following list we've collected some more of the best of the worst—brand names from International Marketing Hell.

Clean Finger Nail	Chinese tissues
Campus Fecund	Japanese notebook paper

Kolic	Japanese mineral water
Suck All—Yone's	Thai bathroom pads
Need Almighty Sucker	
Sanitary Bog: Useful for	Hong Kong ferry bag
containing various dregs and dust.	
Creap creamy powder	Japanese coffee creamer
Last Climax	Japanese tissues
Ass Glue	Chinese glue
Fduhy Sesane	China airlines (CAAC) snack food
Swine	Chinese chocolate
Libido	Chinese soda
Pocari Sweat	Japanese sport drink
Ucc	Japanese coffee
Ban Cock	Indian cockroach repellent
Shocking	Japanese chewing gum
Homo sausage	East Asian fish sausage
Cat Wetty	Japanese moistened hand towels
Hornyphon	Austrian video recorder
Shitto	Ghanaian pepper sauce
Pipi	Yugoslavian orangeade
Polio	Czechoslovakian laundry detergent
Crundy	Japanese gourmet candy
Superglans	Netherlands car wax
I'm Dripper	Japanese instant coffee

Old Beans	Japanese coffee
Zit	Greek soft drink
My Fanny	Japanese toilet paper
Colon Plus	Spanish detergent

On Dancing, Ballroom:

Ballroom dancing has been around in various forms since early civilization, and it has been a crucial factor in the development of mankind.

> *Senator Howell Heflin (D-Alabama), when presenting a resolution to the Senate that would establish National Ballroom Dance Week*

On Dancing, Modern:

Modern dancing is so old-fashioned.

> *movie mogul Samuel Goldwyn*

On Dates, Hot:

What was he doing with Miss Saigon?
> *Buck Showalter, New York Yankee manager, when told that general*
> *manager Gene Michael had gone to see Broadway play* Miss Saigon

On Days:

It's a beautiful day for a night game.
> *Frank Frisch, sportscaster*

On Death:

Please provide the date of your death.
> *IRS letter sent to a dead man whose widow had filed a return for him*

On Death, Serious:

Four people were killed, one seriously, and eight more received slight injuries. . . .
> *from the* Japan Times

On Death, Sort of:

I thought this guy was kind of dead.
> *President George Bush during a meeting with Israeli Prime Minister*
> *Yitzhak Rabin in Maine, when seeing a protester's sign supporting Meir*
> *Kahane, the assassinated right-wing Jewish leader*

On Death, Changeability of:

Your food stamps will be stopped effective March 1992 because we received notice that you passed away. May God bless you. You may reapply if there is a change in your circumstances.

letter from the Greenville, South Carolina, County Department of Social Services

On Death, the First Time Around:

Millions of people who have never died before will be killed.

from a Star Trek *episode, when Captain James T. Kirk falls in love with a woman who is trying to destroy a planet*

On Death, Odd Poetic Images:

We feel that our race is almost run. Like a tired runner, we shall soon cross the harboring bar and, casting aside the harness, shall lie down upon that bourn from whence no traveler returns.

small-town newspaper editor in Wisconsin, mid-1800s, infamous for word-mangling, in his self-written obituary

On the Death Penalty:

Life is indeed precious, and I believe the death penalty helps to affirm this fact.

Edward Koch, New York City mayor

On the Death Penalty:

If the death penalty is to have any kind of future, it needs to be carried out with great reverence and respect for the value of life. Without that respect, we're all killers—no better than the savages.

Joseph Levy, Iowa editor

On Death, Political:

I want to thank each and every one of you for having extinguished yourselves this session.

Gib Lewis, speaker of the Texas House

On Death Takes a Holiday:

We are sorry to announce that Mr. Albert Brown has been quite unwell, owing to his recent death, and is taking a short holiday to recover.

notice in Parish Magazine

On Decapitation:

I thought he was going to dive and decapitate himself . . . badly.

Mike Hendrick, BBC

On Decapitation:

The only luxury is freedom, freedom of the mind. They can chop off my head and take everything else as long as they leave me that.

Dieter Meier, of the rock group Yello

On Decisions:

Today was mostly decision day. We made an agreement to agree over what we had agreed upon before.

Tom Flores, Seahawks general manager

On Decisions:

Reporter: Yogi, have you made up your mind yet?

Yogi Berra: Not that I know of.

On Decisiveness:

Jimmy Hill: Don't sit on the fence, Terry, what chance do you think Germany has of getting through?

Terry Venables (BBC soccer commentator and former manager of soccer team Tottenham (UK) Spurs): I think it's fifty-fifty.

On the Declaration of World War I, Unusual Observations:

And it was this month that my book of poems was coming out here! What attention will it get with this going on? What has happened to England? Why don't they stop the war?

poet Amy Lowell

On the Deficit, Historical Reasons Why It's Bad:

The problem is—the deficit is—or should I say—wait a minute, the spending, or gross national product, forgive me—the spending is roughly 23 to 24 per cent. So that it is in—it what is increasing, while the revenues are staying proportionately the same and what would be the proper amount they should, that we should be taking from the private sector.

> *President Ronald Reagan, spontaneously answering reporter's questions*

On Defining "E Pluribus Unum," Great Vice Presidential Moments in:

Out of one, many.

> *Vice President Al Gore reversing the meaning of "E Pluribus Unum"*
> *(which is "out of many, one") and, in the process, un-uniting the states.*

On Definitions, Important Distinctions:

I think immoral is probably the wrong word to use for [my] acts. I prefer the word unethical.

> *Ivan Boesky, convicted financier, at his divorce trial at Manhattan*
> *Supreme Court, when his ex-wife's attorney asked if his insider trading*
> *(termed "incorrect trading" by Boesky) was immoral*

On Déjà Vu:

It's déjà vu all over again.

> *widely attributed to Yogi Berra*

On Democracy, Attorney General's Definition of:

But when you come right down to the basic elements of why we have a Government, it's a monopoly on power. We decided long ago that rather than have this power in the hands of individuals or groups, it should be in the hands of the Government.

> *William Saxbe, attorney general of the United States, mid-1970s, and Republican senator from Ohio*

On Democracy, What to Watch Out for:

If we [legislators] don't watch our respective tails, the people are going to be running the government.

> *Bill Craven, California state senator, discussing the increase in citizens' initiatives, in which petition signing is used to change laws,* Los Angeles Times, *July 22, 1988*

On Democracy, Republican National Convention Definition of:

We are America. Those other people are not.

> *Republican Party Chairman Rich Bond, at the 1992 Republican National Convention*

On Democracy, Unessentials In:

Q: How soon do you expect Argentina to be returned to democratic government?

President Roberto Eduardo Viola of Argentina, from a Time *magazine interview, September 1982:* We believe we are already within a democratic system. Some factors are still missing, like the expression of the people's will.

On Democrats, Gender of:

Women prefer Democrats to men.

Representative Tony Coelho (D-California)

On Dentistry, Non-Catholic:

Teeth extracted by the latest Methodists.

an advertisement for a dentist in Hong Kong

On Departures, Timely:

Traffic is very heavy at the moment, so if you are thinking of leaving now, you'd better set off a few minutes earlier.

Automobile Association spokesman, on the radio

On Depth, Depth of:

We have deep depth.

Yogi Berra

On Desexigration:

What we are about is moving from androcentric values and behaviors to androgynous or better yet (for consciousness raising) gyandrous health care and societal values. In the process, the health occupations must be desexigrated. . . .

NOW president in a letter to the director of the Center for Women in Medicine

On Desserts, Enticing:

Please try the tarts of the house available for your delight on the trolley.

menu from a Cairo luxury hotel, circa 1940

On Desserts, Political:

I find it interesting how we get carried away by the dogma à la mode.

Representative Lincoln Diaz-Ballart of Florida, on NAFTA

On Desserts, Repetitive:

I'll have a pie à la mode with ice cream.

Johnny Logan, ex-Milwaukee Braves shortstop, when ordering in a restaurant

On Devotion, a Bit Excessive:

McMahon was a friendly, approachable man. . . . He was certainly an odd mixture . . . the fanaticism for physical fitness; the gossipy optimism, and his almost embarrassing pubic display of devotion to his wife, Sonia, and his three children.

> *the* Times of London *obituary for Sir William McMahon, Australian prime minister*

On Dining Out, Options in:

For those of our customers who are vegetables, we are able to offer a plate of hot mixed vegetables.

> *from an Italian restaurant menu, La Patata, in Tokyo*

On Diplomacy, Great Definitions of:

The conduct of international affairs is essentially dialectic, and you have a sine curve of attitudes. We felt there had to some clearing of the air.

> *Secretary of State Alexander Haig, in a* Wall Street Journal *interview*

On Diplomacy, Great Moments in:

I'd like to extend a warm welcome to Chairman Mo.

> *President Ronald Reagan, trying to welcome Liberian President Doe*

On Diplomacy, Great Moments in:

Everybody likes to go to Geneva. I used to do it for the Law of the Sea conferences and you'd find these potentates from down in Africa, you know, rather than eating each other, they'd just come up and get a good square meal in Geneva.

> *Senator Ernest F. Hollings (South Carolina-D), on African diplomats who traveled to Geneva to take part in the just concluded international trade agreement talks*

On Diplomacy, Great Moments in:

I will now open these trousers, and reveal some even more precious treasures to Your Royal Highness.

> *Archbishop of Uppsala, Sweden, trying to impress an English royal visitor with his knowledge of the English*

On Diplomacy, Great Moments in:

And tell me, does your husband have big balls?

> *Lynne Reid Banks, novelist and playwright, to the wife of the Swedish ambassador to England, referring to the social event*

On Diplomacy, Great Moments in:

After the war, France and England should join hands to make a formidable fart.

> *The Duke of Windsor, talking to French troops during World War II, and mistakenly using the masculine article, which changed the meaning of his words*

On Diplomats, Function of:

I'm the consul for information, but I don't have any information.

> *Ofra Ben Yaacoe, Chicago Israeli consul*

On Directions, Clear:

To move the [elevator] cabin, push button of the wishing floor. If the cabin should enter more persons, each one should press the number of wishing floor. Driving is then going alphabetically by natural order. Button retaining pressed position shows received command for visiting station.

elevator directions in a Madrid, Spain, hotel

On Directing, Clear:

Don't do it the way I did it. Do it the way I meant it.

Otto Preminger, director, explaining to Linda Darnell and Cornell Wilde how to do a scene

On Disappointment:

I was very pleasantly disappointed.

movie mogul Samuel Goldwyn

On Discrimination:

We don't necessarily discriminate. We simply exclude certain types of people.

Lieutenant Colonel Gerald Wellman, MIT ROTC instructor, defending the military ban on gays

On Display Ads, Gripping:

Hunt's Scaffolding Services
"Satisfaction with Every Erection"

from an English construction firm ad, displayed on a truck in London

On Distances:

I don't think he's ever lost a race at 200 meters, except at 400.

> *David Coleman, BBC sports commentator, known for his on-air gaffes*
> *called "Colemanballs" in England, covering the 1992 Olympics*

On Dividing:

Pizza counter person: Do you want the pizza cut into six or eight slices?

Dan Osinksi, ballplayer: Better make it six. I can't eat eight.

> *Dan Osinski, former Red Sox pitcher, when asked how many slices he*
> *wanted his pizza cut into (also attributed to Yogi Berra)*

On Dr. Zhivago:

Yogi Berra (after his wife had mentioned she had been to see Doctor Zhivago*):* What's the matter with you now?

On Dogs, Explosive:

1) Recommend clarification of the Plattsburg request, the FSNs used, WRAMA's comments, and FSNs in the TA.

2) There will be a tendency towards confusion unless more or more explicit information is given. AFLC cannot identify any FSN to Dog Detection—Explosive or as WRAMA puts in the 17 Oct 73 letter, Patrol Dog/Explosive. We cannot determine whether they want a dog or an explosive. . . .

> *Department of the Air Force memo, Aerospace Equipment Division*

On Dogs vs. Humans, Parachuting:

We have soldiers here in training jumping every day, but we wouldn't consider jumping the dogs that often. It's an expensive proposition to train the dogs and we don't want to take unnecessary risks with them,

Fort Bragg, North Carolina, spokesman, explaining why the Army intended to restrict the use of parachuting dogs

On Doing What's Right No Matter What, Politicians and:

I'm not going to come out with programs that will defeat me, no matter how I stand on that program, because I want to get elected. There may be some programs that you believe in and I believe in that will not be campaign issues, because if they are, I won't be governor.

R. B. Jordan III, lieutenant governor, running for Democratic nomination for governor of North Carolina, as reported in Raleigh News and Observer

On Driving:

Two vehicles which are passing each other in opposite directions shall have the right of way.

Article 6, Paragraph 82, Subsection Division 3, New York State Vehicle and Traffic Law

On Economist/Ambassador John Kenneth Galbraith, Little-Known Facts About:

I remember him. Short guy, mustache, played third base for Pittsburgh.

> *Jackie Moore, Toronto Blue Jay player, after being told that economist John Kenneth Galbraith was on the same flight*

On Economizing:

Spare no expense to make everything as economical as possible.

> *movie mogul Samuel Goldwyn*

On Education:

We're going to have the best-educated American people in the world.

Vice President Dan Quayle

On Education:

Extant data systems contain an abundance of knowledge which is underutilized due to deficit of knowledge and abilities due to inaccessibility.

from a New York City Board of Education memo, explaining that there was a great deal of information available that they couldn't understand or use

On Education, Problems with:

Too many textbooks and discussions leave students free to make up their minds about things.

Mel Gabler, Texas textbook criticizer

On Education, Reinventing:

We need energies and synergies to develop agendas.

Janie Hatton, Principal of the Year and principal of Trade and Technical High School, Milwaukee, Wisconsin, explaining the advice she would give President Clinton on how to improve schools

On Education, Why We Need:

Function I of education is to continue by a definite program, though in a diminishing degree, the integration of students. . . . Function III is to reveal higher activities of an increasingly differentiated type in the major fields of experience and culture and their significance. . . . Function V is to systemize knowledge in such ways as to show its significance and especially of the laws and principles.

> *The Report of the Committee on the Orientation of Secondary Education, 1940*

On Egg-Laying, Advice on:

The right honorable gentleman has done what I would like you all to do—when you lay an egg, put it by for a rainy day.

> *R. Thwiates, Conservative candidate, 1880*

On Ego:

As God once said, and I think rightly . . .

> *Field Marshall Bernard Law Montgomery, British war hero, (apocryphal)*

On Eight-Day Weeks:

Open seven days a week, excluding Sundays!

> *Sign on a Kentucky Fried Chicken store*

On Elections, Great Insights on:

The only way that the Republican Party can hold the White House . . . is to nominate a candidate who can win.

> *Alexander Haig, former Secretary of State and pundit*

On Elm Beetles, Virility of:

Elm Beetle Infestation Ravishing Thousands of Trees in Greenwich.
New York Times headline, cited by Theodore Bernstein (1904–1979)
in his "Winners and Sinners" Bulletin he distributed to fellow Times
staffers. He titled this headline and discussion "Insex."

On Emergency Services, Overly Helpful:

Youth hit by Train is rushed to Two Hospitals.
Observer *headline*

On Employees, Clean and Boxed:

We are specializing in making dried-pork and pork-sliced. . . . The
staff is under expert supervision and hygienically packed.
Hong Kong dried pork package

On the End of the Rainbow, What to Find:

And this is the real carrot at the end of the rainbow.
Paul Lyneham, ABC-TV, Australia

On Endorsements:

All I was doing was appealing for an endorsement, not suggesting
you endorse it.
President George Bush, to Colorado Governor Roy Romer

On English:

Ol' Diz knows the king's English. And not only that, I also know the queen is English.

Dizzy Dean, baseball great, on air responding to a letter from a listener that said he didn't know the King's English

On English Idioms, Well-Known:

To use an English phrase, he is a host in himself.

from the English-Chinese Word Ocean Dictionary

On English Idioms, Well-Known:

I am not wanting to make too long speech tonight as I am knowing your old English saying, "Early to bed and up with the cock."

Hungarian diplomat, in a speech to an embassy party

On Environmental Careers for Gals, Etc.:

They'll hire girls too, and handicapped people will find jobs if they qualify.

from Popeye and Environmental Careers, *a school handbook for young people considering careers in science and the environment*

On Environmentalists, Great:

We don't have to worry about endangered species—why, we can't even get rid of the cockroach.

James Watt, Secretary of the Interior in the Reagan administration

On Epitaphs, Great:

> Here lies John Higley, whose father and mother were
> drowned in their passage from America.
> Had they both lived, they would have been buried here.
> *Irish gravestone epitaph, supposedly at Belturbet, Ireland*

On Epitaphs, Great:

Here lyes the Bodeys of George Young and Isobel Gutherie and all their Posterity for more than fifty years backwards.

> *British gravestone epitaph, reported in 1757*

On the Equal Rights Amendment:

It is about a socialist, anti-family political movement that encourages women to leave their husbands, kill their children, practice witchcraft, destroy capitalism and become lesbians.

> *Pat Robertson, religious leader and (at the time) presidential hopeful, on the proposed ERA in Iowa*

On Etiquette, Dining:

When we sit down to dinner we are obliged to keep both hands armed.

> *Sir Boyle Roche, eighteenth century member of Parliament from Tralee, famed for his word mangling*

On Etiquette, Great Moments in:

Sir John Gielgud discussing a mutual acquaintance with a friend, E.K.: "Oh, I know, but he's such a *bore!* He's almost as big a bore as E.K.!"

On Europe, Definitive Word on:

The people don't take baths and they don't speak English. No golf courses, no room service. Who needs it?

Jim McMahon, Chicago Bears quarterback

On Evolution, Basketball:

I didn't develop as a basketball player. I evolved. First, I was a defensive specialist. Then, I incorporated the shot blocking and then I threw the dunking and jump shooting into the mix. I came up with a dominating, exterminating, germinating, postulating, machine.

Edgar Jones, former San Antonio Spurs player

On Experts, Always Right Division:

In the opinion of competent experts it is idle to look for a commercial future for the flying machine. There is, and always will be, a limit to its carrying capacity. . . . Some will argue that because a machine will carry two people, another may be constructed that will carry a dozen, but those who make this contention do not understand the theory.

W. J. Jackman and Thomas Russell, Flying Machines: Construction and Operation, *1910.*

On Experts, Always Right Division:

The atomic bomb will not go off. And I speak as an expert in explosives.

Admiral W. Leahy to President Truman, 1945

On Expressions:

There's a very sad-looking Wattana, but you'd never know it to look at his face.

Ted Lowe, British sportscaster

On Extortion, Why Idaho Wants You to Be Good at:

Every person who unsuccessfully attempts, by means of any verbal threat, to extort money or other property, from another is guilty of a misdemeanor.

Idaho Code, 1932, Section 17-3897

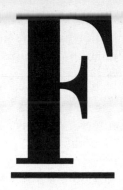

On Failure:

These people haven't seen the last of my face. If I go down, I'm going down standing up.

Chuck Person, Indiana Pacers player, after his team fell two games behind the Boston Celtics in the NBA playoffs

On Failure:

John didn't flunk his physical, he just didn't pass it.

Steve Ortmayer, San Diego Chargers manager

On Family, Broad Definition of:

I've done everything from horses down to chicken, hogs, cats, and goats. I've treated them all, including members of my family.

acupuncturist H. Grady Young

On the Family, Last Word on:

I've been blessed with wonderful parents and a wonderful family and I am proud of my family. Anybody turns to their family. I have a very good family. I'm very fortunate to have a very good family. I believe very strongly in the family. It's one of the things we have in our platform to talk about.

Vice President Dan Quayle. (His father said about him: "He doesn't have the greatest smarts in the world.")

On Famous Lines:

Cheered by their words and with an altogether more positive attitude to boxing . . . I found myself recalling the words of Marlon Brando in *On the Waterfront*, "I could have been a bartender."

Alex Hendy and Akwi Seo in Look Japan, *an English language magazine in Tokyo*

On Fans:

If the people don't want to come out to the park, nobody's going to stop them.

Yogi Berra, explaining why fan attendance was dropping at Kansas City

On Fans, Mets:

These fans are very rabid like they were very collegiate or something because it takes four hours for us to leave our dressing room after a game, which is good because the concessions people sell a lot of hot dogs, which is good for our business and I like that. I expect that very soon they will carry one of my players out on their shoulders like he just caught the winning touchdown for Yale. They are very patient and that's good. These fellows of ours are going to keep improving because they are better than most folks think and not as bad as they used to be. Because it would be hard to be as bad as that.

Casey Stengel, Mets manager and baseball great, talking about the Mets fans, as quoted in Sporting News, *October 18, 1975*

On Fans, Toothsome:

Those amateur umpires are certainly flexing their fangs tonight.

Jerry Coleman, San Diego Padres announcer

On Farm Policy, Dan Quayle's Detailed Knowledge of:

Target prices? How that works? I know quite a bit about farm policy. I come from Indiana, which is a farm state. Deficiency payments, which are the key—that is what gets the money into the farmer's hands. We got loan, uh, rates, we get target, uh, prices, uh, I have worked very closely with my senior colleague, Richard Lugar, making sure that the farmers of Indiana are taken care of.

> *Vice President Dan Quayle, during a press conference, in response to a reporter's request that he define the term "target prices." (After this question, Quayle's press secretary called an end to the conference—making the press conference only two minutes and thirty seconds.)*

On Fast-Food Joints, Beverage Choices in:

Counter person at McDonald's: What do you want to drink?
James Buckley, aristocratic candidate for senator: What's your house Chablis?

On Feathered Cattle:

Owners of such grass fields could then rear cattle or other poultry on their land.

> *unnamed Malaysian state minister, on the advantages of planting grass in idle rural areas, quoted in the* Far Eastern Economic Review

On Fiction, Problem with:

Simplifying grossly, an aceteme is a single narrative unit or chunk in a (not necessarily) fictional discourse, a unit generated by language but subsequently capable of resonating in the reader's mind in a free-floating, extra-linguistic form. And if I revive the concept here, just a week after the brouhaha surrounding the presentation of the 20 Best Young Novelists of 1992, it's because it increasingly seems to me that what is wrong with contemporary British Fiction is its chronic shortage of memorable and enduring actemes.

Gilbert Adair, in the Sunday Times of London

On Fiction, Problem with:

This book has too much plot and not enough story.

movie mogul Samuel Goldwyn

On Fiction Writing, Definitive Words on:

Fiction writing is great. You can make up almost anything.

Ivana Trump, after writing her first novel

On Fielding, Minor Problems with:

The only problem I really have in the outfield is with fly balls.

Carmelo Martinez, San Diego Padres outfielder

On Fifty-Fifty:

I want this to be fifty-fifty like I said. But I want you to see that I get the best part of it.

movie mogul Samuel Goldwyn

On the Fifty-Second State:

I was asked to come to Chicago because Chicago is one of our fifty-two states.

> *Raquel Welch, on her appearance at a pro-choice rally in Chicago, on "Larry King Live"*

On 53–0 Losses, Good Explanations for:

If we hadn't given them those first four touchdowns, it might have been different.

> *Hokes Bluff, Alabama, high school football coach H. K. "Cootie" Reeves, when his team lost 53–0 in the state Double A title game*

On Fighter Pilots, Virility of:

The pilot of the fighter, identified as Captain Kim Yong-bae, was reported to have ejaculated shortly before the crash to safety and was evacuated to a nearby military hospital.

> Korea Times *item*

On Film, Cultural Contributions of:

Ordinary rape and murder just doesn't make it any more. It's much better to have ultra-violence, chainsaw massacres, X-rated Draculas, and continents sinking into the sea with the entire population lost, at the very least.

> *Jon Davidson, advertising and PR chief at New World pictures*

On Films, Botto:

Sabotage: An extremely enjoyable film for young and old that will shake your bottoms.

> *advertisement for an indian film*

On Films, Great Names of:

After the Balled-Up Ball
> *1915 American film*

On Films, Great Names of:

Who Created the YoYo? Who Created the Moon Buggy?
> *1980 Philippine film*

On Films, Great Names of:

The Heart of a Lady as Pure as a Full Moon Over the Place of Medical Salvation
> *1955 American Film* Not as a Stranger *as titled in Hong Kong*

On Finality:

I was unhappy . . . but it's over, done, water under the dam.
> *Cal Ripkin, Sr., baseball manager, upon being fired*

On Fire, Great Thoughts on:

Most fires are caused by some igniting source coming into contact with combustible material.
> *official definition, from the Department of Technical Cooperation, Departmental Fire Precautions*

On First Jobs:

It was just a job. It wasn't any special interest in consumer affairs. I needed a paycheck and the attorney general said that I would be the best to go down there, because he knew that I was anticonsumer.

> *Vice President Dan Quayle on how he got his first job—at the consumer protection division of the Indiana attorney general's office*

On First Ladies, Little-Known Habits of:

I didn't intend for this to take on a political tone. I'm just here for the drugs.

> *Nancy Reagan, former first lady, when asked a political question while at a "Just Say No" rally.*

On First-Rate Scientists, Value of:

Two second-rate scientists are as good as one first-rate one.

> *James Ionson, director of a division of the Pentagon Strategic Defense Initiative, commenting on the boycott by many top scientists*

On Flags:

. . . if Berger gets another yellow flag, it will be a red one.

> *David Coleman, BBC sports commentator, known for his on-air gaffes called "Colemanballs" in England, covering the 1992 Olympics*

On Flight Attendants, Excessively Familiar:

Stewardess during flight: Sir, Would you like some sauce on your balls?

> *quoted in a local article enjoining flight attendants for Singapore Airlines to learn better English*

On Florida — Grown Strawberry Lobby, Strength of:

The first proviso of section 8c(6)(I) of the Agricultural Adjustment Act (7 U.S.C. 608c(6)(I), reenacted with amendments by the Agricultural Marketing Agreement Act of 1937, is amended by striking out "or tomatoes" and inserting in lieu thereof "tomatoes, or Florida grown strawberries."

> *part of the Trade Bill in the Senate, Section 4602*

On Focus:

I don't think there's anybody in this organization not focused on the 49ers—I mean Chargers.

> *Bill Belchick, Cleveland Browns coach, on his team's preparation for an upcoming game with the San Diego Chargers*

On Food Subsidies for Congressmen, Reasons for:

On the basis that it is essential and economical, economical for the country and for the Congress to have food available around here.

> *Representative Jamie L. Whitten, (D-Mich.) on why food subsidies were being cut for the poor—but kept for the House and Senate restaurants*

On Foot Ball:

Men, I want you just thinking of one word all season. One word and one word only: Super Bowl.

Ex-Houston Oiler and Florida State coach Bill Peterson

On Football, Great Thoughts About:

The receivers are an integral part of the passing game.

Hank Stram, TV sportscaster

On Football, High Moral Standard of:

I never set out to hurt anybody deliberately unless it was, you know, important. Like a league game or something.

Dick Butkus, linebacker and Hall of Famer

On Football, Personal Sacrifices for:

I am the youngest grandson of the Paramount Chief of American Samoa and as such I was the heir to the throne, but when I was chosen as Captain of the North Carolina State Football Team, I had to decide between football and politics. I chose football. My uncle became Ruler for Life. It really hits me when I am alone.

Captain Logo, captain of the North Carolina State football team

On Foreign Policy, Great Moments in:

It may be necessary to kill half the Filipinos in order that the remaining half may be advanced to a higher plane of life than their present semi-barbarous state affords.

General Shafter, U.S. general in charge of subduing the Philippines in 1900

On Fortunes, Odd Definitions of:

He was a poor boy, who, entirely through hard work and brains, worked his way up to within a few cents of a fabulous fortune.

> *Mayor of San Francisco in the 1960s, at a banquet for a local boy, reported by Leo Rosten*

On Four-Letter Words:

You won't find a single four-letter word in there. I don't go for that bullshit.

> *Bob Feller, Hall of Fame pitcher, talking about his autobiography*

On Fraternal Organizations, Little-Known Facts About:

Jesus Christ is the greatest Rotarian.

> *Reverend Howard S. Williams, D.D., speaking before Chicago Rotarians*

If Jesus Christ was on earth today, He would be a Shriner.

> *Reverend J. Whitcomb Brougher, D.D., of the Temple Baptist Church, Los Angeles, circa 1925*

God was the first Kiwanian.

> *Reverend W. F. Powell, speaking before the Kiwanis Club of Columbus*

There was one 100% Rotarian. He lived 2000 years ago. His name was Jesus Christ.

> *Henry Dodge, speaking at the Wilmington Rotary Club*

St. Patrick was the first real Kiwanian of the Celtic race.

Reverend Dr. John F. Johnston, quoted in the Hartford Courant

There must have been something divine in the origin of Rotary.

Charles E. Watkins, speaking at a Jacksonville Rotarian meeting

On Free Services:

Free cholesterol testing will be offered at 10 this morning. The cost is $6.

notice in the Hammond, Indiana, Times, *quoted by Herb Caen in the* San Francisco Chronicle

On Freedom and Individual Ethical Responsibility:

If people get a kick out of running down pedestrians, you have to let them do it.

Paul Jacobs, director of marketing for a company marketing a computerized game called "Death Race" which features cars hitting pedestrians

On Freeze:

Yes, we've got problems at home. And I think I got a good plan to help fix those problems at home. But because of our leadership, because we didn't listen to the freeze—the nuclear freeze group, do you remember, freeze it, back in the 70s, freeze, don't touch it; we're going to lock it in now or else we'll have war.

President George Bush

On French Hospitals, Comforting Words About:

Dr. F. has been appointed to the position of head physician to the Hospital de la Charite. Orders have been issued to the authorities for the immediate extension of the cemetery at Montparnasse.

two stories merged by a French newspaper

On Freudian Slips:

You don't tell us how to stage the news, and we don't tell you how to report it.

Larry Speakes, Bush press secretary, to the press, October 12, 1982

On Freudian Slips, Ted Kennedy and:

She's a wonderful, wonderful person, and we're looking forward to a happy and wonderful night—uh, life.

Ted Kennedy, Massachusetts senator, to the South Shore Chamber of Commerce about his fiancée, Victoria Reggie

On Fried Chicken, Lip-Smacking Boasts About:

Makes your fingers fall off.

Kentucky Fried Chicken ad, as mistranslated abroad

On Frogs, Hypothetical:

If a frog had wings, he wouldn't hit his tail on the ground. Too hypothetical.

> *President George Bush, during his 1992 campaign trip to New Hampshire, about extending unemployment benefits*

On Fun:

Let's have spontaneous fun—and here's how.

> *Singapore's* Straits Times

On the Fun Things in Life:

It's a great thing to have shot down an aircraft. . . . There's no sweeter sound than your torpedo hitting. Some things don't change.

> *Admiral Mark Hill (Ret.) in the* Washington Times *on the downing of two Libyan jets by the United States*

On the Fun Things in Life, Old-Fashioned:

And meanwhile war is drifting the way of all good old glad things. The old-fashioned Christmas, the old-fashioned dance, the bright old days of sleigh rides and the log fires are gone, and with them, alas, dear old war has got to go.

> *from the* Rotarian *magazine, 1932*

On Funerals:

Always go to other people's funerals, otherwise they won't come to yours.

> *Yogi Berra*

On the Future, Present of:

He's the future and the future is now.
> *Jim Coleman, former Assistant United States Attorney, partner of top Philadelphia law firm Ballard Spahr Andrews & Ingersoll, famed for his malaprops, as collected by his colleagues*

On the Future:

Things happen more frequently in the future than they do in the past.
> *Washington governor Booth Gardner*

On the Future:

I'm interested in stories about people as we knew them in the near-recent future.
> *Philip Kaufman,* Star Trek *writer/director*

On the Future, Past of:

We won't see the end result until an hour ago.
> *John Aubuchon, WPIX News reporter, New York, in a report on the Clinton health plan speech*

On Gambling:

Jack, if you ever hear anyone say I am a gambler, contradict it. I never lost a thousand pounds in a night but twice.

Richard Monckton Milnes, First Lord Houghton's father

On Gambling, Great Advice:

Don't forget, folks—The less you bet, the more you lose when you win!

advice from a stickman at the Landmark Casino, Las Vegas

On Games, Old-Fashioned Childhood:

[My daughter loves playing] cowpersons and Indians.

novelist Anne Roiphe

On Gay Rights:

If gays are granted rights, next we'll have to give rights to prostitutes and to people who sleep with St. Bernards and to nailbiters.

Anita Bryant, singer and former spokesperson for Florida orange juice

On Genius:

The word "genius" isn't applicable in football. A genius is a guy like Norman Einstein.

Joe Theisman, ESPN broadcaster and ex-Redskins quarterback. (Theisman later explained to Sports Illustrated *that this was no error; he was referring to a high school classmate of his, Norman Einstein, who graduated at the top of his class.)*

On Geography:

John Barrymore: You should play Hamlet.
Jimmy Durante: To hell with them small towns. I'll stick to New York.

On Geography:

Howard Stern: What is the capital of New York?
Tori Spelling: . . . New Jersey?

Tori Spelling, actress best known for her role in Beverly Hills 90210, *during an on-air radio interview with radio personality Howard Stern*

On Geography:

William, Duke of Gloucester (nephew to King George III), greeting a naval officer: We haven't seen you at court for some time!

Naval officer: Well, no sir; since I was here last I have been nearly to the North Pole.

William: By God, with your red face, you look as if you had been to the *South* Pole.

On the Georgia State Assembly, What They Do in:

Mr. Speaker, will you please turn me on?

> *Georgia State Representative Anne Mueller, complaining to the Georgia speaker Tom Murphy that her microphone was turned off. Speaker Murphy responded: "Thirty years ago, I would have tried."*

On the GNP:

Well, you can't have the gross national product [pause] here's a thing for the return of the people and so forth on that without reflecting those who are paying the taxes.

President Ronald Reagan, quoted in the New York Times

On Goals, Noteworthy:

We expect them [Salvadoran officials] to work toward the elimination of human rights.

Vice President Dan Quayle

On Goats, Escape:

They're just using [the ordinance] as an escape goat.

New Orleans City Councilmember Dorothy Mae Taylor, reacting to news that certain Mardi Gras krewes would stop parading because of the Carnival Public Accommodations Ordinance she sponsored

On God, Little-Known Feats of:

God was the first advertising man.

from a speech given by Reverend Dr. P. H. Martin, as reported in Des Moines Register

On Going Back to the Land, A Simple Way of Life:

The limited cross compliance requirement for the 1987 crop of oats was removed by the Secretary of Agriculture on February 27, 1987. Removing the limited cross-compliance provision for oats permits participation in the wheat, corn and sorghum, cotton, or rice programs even if the acreage of oats intended for grain is in excess of the oat acreage base established for the farm. Limited cross-compliance continues to be in effect for all other program crops, including barley. . . .

USDA letter to farmers

On Going Back to the Land, British-Style:

If you are claiming only Beef Special Premium and/or Suckler Cow Premium *and* are exempted from the stocking density rules, you need not submit an area aid application. You are exempt from the stocking density rules if your total number of Livestock Units (LUs) is not more than 15. This total is based on any milk quota you hold on April 1, 1993, sheep on which you have claimed Sheep Annual Premium in 1993, and cattle on which you are claiming Beef Special Premium or Suckler Cow Premium in 1993. . . . *You will, however, need to submit an area aid application if you wish to claim extensification premium* (see paragraphs 58 to 61 of "CAPO Reform in the Beef Sector").

> *instructions for farmers published by the Ministry of Agriculture, Fisheries, and Food in England, telling farmers how to apply for aid under the European Community's subsidy rules*

On Goings-on:

At present there are such goings on that everything is at a standstill.

> *Sir Boyle Roche, eighteenth century member of Parliament from Tralee, famed for his word mangling*

On Golf, Supreme Importance of:

Golf is second only to Christianity, and is its greatest ally in the development of the highest standard of American manhood and womanhood.

> *Reverend Dr. Paul Arnold Petersen of Pontiac, Michigan, quoted in United Press Dispatch.*

On Colf Caddies, Unknown Duties of:

My horse was in the lead, coming down the homestretch, when the caddie had to fall off.

movie mogul Samuel Goldwyn

On the Good Old Days:

If I were the chief of police, I would get me a hundred good men, give them each a baseball bat, and have them walk down Duval Street and dare one of these freaks to stick his head over the sidewalk. That is the way it was done in Key West in the days I remember and love.

Morris Wright, Baptist minister from Key West, Florida, in a January 1979 ad in a Key West newspaper

On Good Taste, Public Television and:

Considerations of taste made it desirable to use a prop (a banana) instead of the human anatomy to demonstrate the proper use of a condom.

PBS lawyer Nancy Hendry

On Good Weather, Communist Tendencies of:

Under the anti-social capitalist, the great mass of the people are victims of every kind of weather freak . . . the heat parches them and saps their energy and health. Only in the Soviet Union, where there is Socialism, are the rest, leisure and living conditions of the people fully provided for . . . these rights are written into the Stalin Constitution.

from the Soviet-American paper the Daily Worker, *1940*

On Gourmet Cuisine:

Stuffed egg-plant with minced crap.

From a menu at the upscale Jade Garden restaurant in Swire House, Sydney, Australia

On Government Authorizations:

Members of the immediate family of an authorized exchange patron who are not otherwise authorized admission to AAFES-Eur facilities in the company of the authorized patron except for those members of the immediate family who reside in the country where the AAFES-Eur facilities are located.

U.S. Air Force regulation

On the Government, Congressional Knowledge of:

There are four departments. There's the executive, and the legislative, and the judicial, and—the Bill of Rights.

Sen. Kenneth S. Wherry of Nebraska from The Making of a Political Leader: Kenneth S. Wherry and the U.S. Senate, *by Marvin Stromer (1969)*

On Government, Unknown Powers of:

Bill would exempt minors from death.

headline in the North Carolina Goldsboro News Argus

On Government Employees, Female:

All wear attractive uniforms . . . and have interesting jobs with lots of men around.

> *from* Looking Forward to a Career: Government, *career booklet for students, 1975*

On Government's Role in the Insurance Crisis:

For the purpose of this part of the schedule a person over pensionable age, not being an insured person, shall be treated as an employed person if he would be an insured person were he under pensionable age and would be an employed person were he an insured person.

> *from the National Insurance Bill, 1959*

On Government Spending, Why Not?

Funds obligated for military assistance as of September 3, 1979, may, if deobligated, be reobligated.

> *Budget of the United States, fiscal 1980*

On Gratitude:

I will perish this forever.

> *Johnny Logan, shortstop turned sportscaster, upon receiving an award*

On Greatness:

All my shows are great. Some of them are bad. But they are all great.

> *Lew Grade, British producer and media tycoon*

On Gun Control: Why it's Tough in Idaho:

The carrying of concealed weapons is forbidden unless same are exhibited to public view.

Pocatello, Idaho law, 1912

On Guys:

We're all sad to see Glenn Beckert leave. Before he goes, though, I hope he stops by so we can kiss him good-bye. He's that kind of guy.

Jerry Coleman, San Diego Padres announcer

On Gyrations, Political:

Botha is sitting on the rail, with his ear to the ground, listening to see which way the cat will jump.

during a debate in South Africa, about P. W. Botha, South African prime minister

SPECIAL SECTION:
The Stupidest Bad Excuses

Excuses, excuses.

Everyone makes mistakes. And everyone makes excuses. Beginning in childhood, we learn the wonderful art of blaming it all on the other guy, on the weather, on the dog . . .

The problem is, nine times out of ten those excuses sound ridiculously lame.

The stickier the situation, it seems, the weaker the excuse. Take

Gary Hart, for example. He is running for president, he gets caught in a shot with a blonde on his lap, and he quickly starts explaining:

It was suggested I have this picture taken with Miss Rice. This attractive lady whom I had only recently been introduced to dropped into my lap. I was embarrassed. I chose not to dump her off and the picture was taken.

Uh-huh.

Of course, you can't blame him for trying. That's what excuses are for—they're a last-ditch effort to save face, to make yourself seem blameless or at least misunderstood.

And since they're last-ditch efforts, more often than not you wind up making yourself look even worse than you did before. The best policy, of course, is to face up to the mistakes you make—and be a Harry (The Buck Stops Here) Truman. But particularly nowadays, who wants to do that?

After all, if George Washington were alive today, he wouldn't accept the blame for chopping down the cherry tree. He'd blame it on poor parenting.

Some of the Best Bad Excuses:

On Crimes:

I haven't committed a crime. What I did was fail to comply with the law.
David Dinkins, New York City mayor, answering accusations that he failed to pay his taxes

On Not Paying Taxes:

[Paying taxes] was one of the things I was always going to take care of, but sometimes I did not have all the funds available or I did not have all the documents and other materials I needed.

> *David Dinkins, New York City mayor, still trying to answer accusations that he failed to pay his taxes*

On Potentially Politically Incorrect Statements About the Japanese Made by a (Current) President:

I think that the specific comment was a broad general observation followed up by a specific finish to the sentence where he said in this case that he believes Prime Minister Miyazawa means to keep the commitment.

> *George Stephanopolous, Clinton press secretary, clearing up an incident that occurred in a 1993 summit—in which President Clinton passed a note to Russian President Boris Yeltsin reading, "When the Japanese say yes to us, they often mean no"*

On Potentially Politically Incorrect Statements About Blacks Made by a Jurist:

I may have said something about the NAACP being un-American or communist, but I meant no harm by it.

> *Jefferson B. Sessions III, judge*

On Overdrawing Your House of Representatives Bank Account:

They gave you a book of checks. They didn't ask for any deposits.

> *Congressman Joe Early (D-Mass.), at a press conference to answer questions about the House bank scandal*

On Breaking Campaign Pledges by a (Former) President:

He didn't say that. He read what was given to him in a speech.

> *Richard Darman, director of the Office of Management and Budget, explaining why President Bush wasn't following up on his campaign pledge that there would be no loss of wetlands*

On Sleeping on the Job at a Nuclear Power Plant:

It depends on your definition of asleep. They weren't stretched out. They had their eyes closed. They were seated at their desks with their heads in a nodding position.

> *Commonwealth Edison supervisor of news information John Hogan, responding to a charge by a Nuclear Regulatory Commission inspector that two Dresden Nuclear Plant operators were sleeping on the job*

On Losing a Political Debate:

I deliberately fumbled around and didn't do as good as I could. I know that no one remembers what happens in the last two weeks. I gave that guy a false sense of security and he fell for it hook, line, and sinker.

> *Edward G. Edwards, during his campaign for Louisiana governor, 1992*

On Distinctions, Critical:

I didn't accept it. I received it.

> *Richard Allen, National Security Advisor to President Reagan, explaining the $1000 in cash and two watches he was given by two Japanese journalists after he helped arrange a private interview for them with First Lady Nancy Reagan*

On Spying:

I was a pilot flying an airplane and it just so happened that *where* I was flying made what I was doing spying.

> *Francis Gary Powers, U-2 reconnaissance pilot held by the Soviets for spying, in an interview after he was returned to the United States*

On Leaving Incriminating Tape Recordings in the Oval Office:

I was under medication when I made the decision not to burn the tapes.

> *President Richard Nixon*

On Hair:

Don't fix your hair—it's nice if it's loosey.
Michael Curtiz, movie director, to Olivia DeHavilland

On Hair, Academics and:

Black hair has interacted with society, and today I'm trying to make it into a field. You wouldn't find the same interaction in Africa. You don't find the conflict—over whose hair should be what, in what dimensions. . . .

The term itself is homogeneous. It allows people to avoid what black hair is. This is a very real issue, that there is this thing that we are assuming is called "black hair."

> *Professor Kennell Jackson, Stanford University professor and teacher of an upper-level history seminar "Black Hair as Culture and History," which addresses how black hair has "interacted with the black presence in this country"*

On Hair, Politically Correct References to:

Clayton Williams, Republican candidate for governor of Texas: I sure do like your pigtails.

Native American Director of the Inter-Tribal Center: This is a traditional hairstyle and we call them braids.

Williams: Well, I think your pigtails are real cute.

On Haircutters, Political Importance of Foreign:

I mean, he [Christophe] comes from Belgium, so it's important to get him to participate.

> *Harry Thomason, television producer and close friend of President Bill Clinton, explaining why it was important for Clinton to stop traffic at Los Angeles Airport for several hours to get a haircut from hairdresser to the stars, Christophe*

On *Hamlet*, Memorability of:

Harry Cohn (movie mogul): I want a speech that every person in the audience will recognize immediately.

Screenwriter of Spartacus: You mean like Hamlet's soliloquy?

Cohn: No! No! I mean something like "To be or not to be."

On *Hamlet*, Reasons to Like:

I mean, it's a great story. It's got some great things in it. I mean, there's something like eight violent deaths.

actor Mel Gibson, in a school video explaining Hamlet

On the Handicapped, Sensitivity to:

And now, will y'all stand and be recognized?

Gib Lewis, Texas Speaker of the House, on Disability Day, to a group of people in wheelchairs watching the House session

On Hands, Growing and Talking:

I recognize the hand that crops up in this veto. I have heard it before.

unnamed congressman during congressional debate

On Hanoi, Improvements in:

Hanoi Unveils Larger Dong.

headline in the Phnom Penh Post. *(The dong is the Vietnamese unit of currency.)*

On Happiness:

Dorothy Macmillan: What are you looking forward to now?
Madame DeGaulle: A penis.
[shocked silence]
General DeGaulle: My dear, I think the English don't pronounce the word quite like that. It's not "a penis" but "'appiness."

> *exchange at a French dinner party at the time of General DeGaulle's retirement, as quoted in* Robert Morley's Book of Bricks, *by Robert Morley*

On Happiness:

If I could drop dead right now, I'd be the happiest man alive.

> *movie mogul Samuel Goldwyn*

On Happiness:

You know Earl. He's not happy unless he's not happy.

> *Elrod Hendricks, former Baltimore Orioles player, talking about fomer Baltimore Orioles manager Earl Weaver (as quoted in Ron Luciano's* The Umpire Strikes Back)

On Happiness:

I feel my best when I'm happy.

> *Winona Ryder, actress, in* New Woman *magazine*

On Harvard Business School, What You Don't Learn at:

The practice of assassination is universally ignored by guides to ... modern management theory; it is, however, alive and thriving ... in Thailand, and stands as evidence of ... the reality that not every problem can be solved by face-to-face bargaining.

> *Robert Cooper, in his* The Foreign Businessman's Guide to Doing Business in Thailand

On Hawaii, Vice Presidential Observations on:

Hawaii is a unique state. It is a small state. It is a state that is by itself. It is a—it is different that the other 49 states. Well, all states are different, but it's got a particularly unique situation.

> *Vice President Dan Quayle, answering a question about the universal health-care plan in Hawaii*

On Health:

I've been healthy my whole career except for a few nagging injuries the last few years.

> *Mike Smith, Cincinnati Reds relief pitcher*

On Health, Why Modern Sports Players Are in Better:

Arabic exercises.

> *Curt Gowdy, giving his view as to why modern sports players have longer careers than in the past*

On Heat:

An oppressive heat wave passed over Calcutta yesterday. In the city the temperature rose to the record figure of about 108 degrees. This sudden rise of temperature was responsible for the intolerable heat.

from a Malaysian newspaper

On Heaven, Details About:

Heaven is a city 15,000 miles square or 6000 miles around. One side is 245 miles longer than the length of the Great Wall of China. Walls surrounding Heaven are 396,000 times higher than the Great Wall of China and eight times as thick. Heaven has twelve gates, three on each side and has room for 100,000,000,000 souls. There are no slums. The entire city is built of diamond material, and the streets are paved with gold. All inhabitants are honest and there are no locks, no courts, and no policemen.

Reverend Dr. George Hawes, of Harrisburg, Pennsylvania, as quoted in the Harrisburg Evening News

On Heaven, How It's Organized:

The Kingdom of Heaven is like a football squad, which is assembled under a coach who formed it into a team that moved with such order and precision, in startling innovation, that it subdued all its opponents.

sermon by Reverend Larry Christenson at Notre Dame University football stadium

On Heaven, What to Expect:

Baseball will be taught in Heaven.

> *Dr. John Howard Dikasen, speaking before the Uniontown, Pennsylvania, Kiwanis Club*

On Height:

The Minutemen are not tall in terms of height.

> *Dan Bonner, CBS sportscaster, covering a University of Massachusetts–Penn State basketball game*

On Help-Wanted Ads:

WANTED:

Hyundai Interpretation School would like a spoken English instructor as follows:

- Qualifications:

B.A. degree or higher

- Sex: Male or Female

(preferred)

> *from the Help-Wanted section of the* Korea Times

On Help-Wanted Ads:

Company Secretary Finance Manager.

1) Half-grey haired executives

2) Must be waist-deep in their field of activities.

3) Must be having the know-how and the do-how of the latest developments in their respective fields.

Sales Manager, Area Sales Manager

4) Must go the whole hog-hug to keep things going.

from the Appointments Vacant section of Business India

On Helpful Hints:

Caution: Blade is extremely sharp! Keep out of Children!

warning on knife blade manufactured by Olfa Corporation, winner of the Dunce Award, by the U.S. Society for the Preservation of English Language and Literature (SPELL)

On Helpful Hints:

Make sure hands, etc. are inside before closing windows.

from 1992 Nissan owner's manual

On Helpful Hints, Governmental:

Q: What should I do if I find a rock in a bag of potatoes?

A: Simply return the rock to your grocer, who will give you the rock's weight in potatoes.

from a U.S. Department of Agriculture booklet, How to Buy Potatoes

On Helpful Hints, Important Governmental:

Persons in contact with iguanas should practice strict hand washing.

bulletin from the Centers for Disease Control, on salmonella prevention

On Ernest Hemingway:

Friend: Have you ever heard of Ernest Hemingway?

Yogi Berra: I don't think so. What paper does he write for?

On High Moral Principle, Dow Chemical and:

We hung in on napalm when it didn't mean anything to us business-wise. The Government asked us to make it and we did. We believed in the principle.

Dow Chemical Company president on how he is "sick and tired of the chemical industry being picked on"

On Holidays:

Because of the Veteran's day holiday next Wednesday, this release will be published on Friday, November 13, instead of on Thursday, November 12. It will be issued on Thursday, November 19, its usual publication date, but will be delayed the following week until Friday, November 17, because of the Thanksgiving Day holiday on Thursday, November 26.

Federal Reserve memo, quoted in the Washington Monthly, *December 1992*

On Hollywood:

The trouble with this business is the dearth of bad pictures.

movie mogul Samuel Goldwyn

On Hotel Bills:

I'm here to pay my accidentals.

Mike Smith, Cincinnati Reds relief pitcher, paying incidental expenses at a hotel desk

On Hotel Management:

Please deposit your valuables in the management.

room card at Guangdong Victory Hotel, Guangdong (Canton) China

On Hotel Mottos, Unusual:

Serve you with Hostiality.

from the Fu Hua and East Lake Hotels, Guangdong (Canton) province, China

On Hotels, Dualistic:

The nearest hotel was five miles away in one direction and practically 12 miles in the opposite direction.

from a travel article in the Irish Ulster Magazine

On Hotels, Little Extras that Make the Difference in:

The hotel is patrolled by security guards, however, the Management advises all guests to make full use of the spy.

from the Nanlin Hotel, Suzhou, China, handout to guests

On Housing, Unusual:

We will always have people [who are] wealthy and have a condom in the south of France.

Caroline Miller, Oregon county commissioner

On Humans, Problems of Identifying:

This means that we have to invent new conceptual artificialities in order to give an account of what we see when we meet somebody who looks and behaves like a human being. How do we know that he is one?

Professor Niklas Luhmann, Reconstructing Individualism

On IBM:

I think there is a world market for about five computers.
Thomas J. Watson, IBM, in 1958

On Ideal Sex, Why Women Like It More than Men:

The purpose of sex ideally is for the woman to attain orgasm and for the man not to.
Sting, rock star, in a Rolling Stone *interview*

On Identity:

Casey Stengel: I won't trade my left fielder.

Reporter: Who's your left fielder?

Stengel: I don't know, but if it isn't him, I'll keep him anyway.

On Ignorance and Apathy, Whether Bad Playing Was Due to:

I don't know and I don't care.

> *Jeff Wilkens, Utah Jazz forward, when asked by his coach Frank Lay-*
> *dern whether his bad playing in a game was due to ignorance or apathy*

On Ignorance and Ronald Reagan:

. . . we wanted to be sure that the President could honestly deny that he had any idea what was going on here.

> *Deputy Treasury Secretary R. T. McNamara, on why Reagan was kept*
> *in the dark on tax reform plans*

On Immortality, Loan Guarantees and:

So long as any amount shall remain unpaid under this Note, the Borrower covenants and promises to the Bank that the Borrower will not permit or suffer to exist any of the following conditions: (a) death of the Borrower.

> *a loan agreement form at the American Security Bank, in Washington*
> *D.C., quoted in* Reader's Digest, *May 1993, from* Fortune

On Improvement:

The places where I need work are on my inside and outside games.

> *Darnell Hillman, Kansas City Kings player*

On Improvements, Strange:

He would not rest satisfied until the rocky mountains of Ireland became cultivated valleys.

> *Sir Boyle Roche, eighteenth century member of Parliament from Tralee, famed for his word mangling, praising another politician's efforts to improve the lot of Ireland*

On Incest, Congressional Wisdom About:

With incest, you could get super-smart kids.

> *Representative Carl Gunter, (R-La.)*

On Inflexibility, Flexible:

It is precisely in order to safeguard democracy and liberty that today more than ever it is necessary to be inflexible.

> *Augusto Pinochet, president of Chile, 1984*

On Information, Surprising:

The speedometer measures speed.

> *from a 1992 Nissan owners manual*

On Innocent Civilians, Why You Can Bomb 'Em:

The definition of "innocents" gets to be a little bit unclear. They do live there, and ultimately the people have some control over what goes on in their country.

> *senior U.S. Air Force official on the civilian death toll in the Gulf War, quoted in the* Progessive

On Instructions, Helpful.

How to store your baby walker: First, remove baby. . . .
instructions included with a baby walker

On Instructions:

Go see it and see for yourself why you shouldn't go see it.
movie mogul Samuel Goldwyn

On Integrity:

I believe in editorial integrity, but a lot of people have old-fashioned ideas of what integrity means.
Robert Cohen, magazine consultant

On Integrity, Criminal:

Early voluntary disclosure, coupled with full cooperation and complete access to necessary records are strong indications of contractor integrity, even in the wake of disclosures of potential criminal liability.
Deputy Secretary of Defense William Taft IV, to military contractors

On Integrity, Senatorial:

Thank you for contacting me to express your opposition . . . to the early use of military by the US against Iraq. I share your concerns. On January 11, I voted in favor of a resolution that would have insisted that economic sanctions be given more time to work and against a resolution giving the president the immediate authority to go to war.
January 22, 1991, letter from Senator John Kerry (D-Mass.) to a constituent

Thank you for contacting me to express your support for the actions of President Bush in response to the Iraqi invasion of Kuwait. From the outset of the invasion, I have strongly and unequivocally supported President Bush's response to the crises and the policy goals he has established with our military deployment in the Persian Gulf.

> *January 31, 1991, letter from Senator John Kerry (D-Mass.) to the* same *constituent*

On Intelligence, Military:

We must not be misled to our own detriment to assume that the untried machine can displace the proved and tried horse.

> *Major General John H. Herr, in 1938. Several years later, World War II began with tanks, fighter planes, aircraft carriers, etc. Horses were not decisive.*

On Interviewing, Great Moments in:

Reporter: Where did the fire start?
Prince Andrew, Duke of York: It started in the Private Chapel.
Reporter: What's that called?
Prince Andrew: The Private Chapel.

> *as reported in* Private Eye, *December 18, 1992*

On Interviewing, Great Moments in:

Jimmy Hill, BBC soccer commentator: But you said it should have been a goal.

Terry Venables, former soccer manager for the Tottenham (UK) Spurs: No, I didn't. I said it should have been a goal.

Jimmy Hill: So you've changed your tune then.

On Introductions, Gracious:

New York hostess introducing Prince Yussupov, Russian royal who killed Rasputin, an evil priest who was gaining control of the government: This is Prince Rasputin, who murdered—Just who was it you *did* murder, Prince Rasputin?

On Investment Know-how:

It's better to buy a $1 stock if it goes up 100%, than to buy a $50 stock that will go up 100%.

> *Jim Coleman, former Assistant United States Attorney, partner of top Philadelphia law firm Ballard Spahr Andrews & Ingersoll, famed for his malaprops, as collected by his colleagues*

On Investment Know-how:

Nothing has come along to beat the horse and buggy.

> *Chauncy Depew, businessman, to his nephew about to invest in a little company named Ford Motor*

On IQs, Telling Comments About:

Sure I've got one. It's a perfect twenty-twenty.

> *Duane Thomas, Dallas Cowboys halfback, answering a question on whether he had an IQ*

On Invitations, Gracious:

Reverend William Spooner: I want you to come to tea next Thursday to meet Mr. Casson.

Mr. Casson: But I *am* Mr. Casson.

Dr. Spooner: Come all the same.

> *Reverend William Spooner, Oxford academic, famed for his tongue-twisting malaprops, called "spoonerisms"*

On the Irish:

Mr. Kanso Yoshida, cousin of the Emperor Hirohito of Japan, has died in Liverpool aged 78. Since he came to Liverpool in 1912, Mr. Yoshida has been known as Paddy Murphy.

> *item in the* Liverpool Free Press, *July 29, 1973*

On the IRS, Comforting Thoughts About:

You will find it a distinct help . . . if you know and look as if you know what you are doing.

> *IRS training manual for tax auditors*

On the IRS, Wisdom of:

Passive activity income does not include the following: Income for an activity that is not a passive activity.

> *IRS Form 8583, Passive Activity Loss Limitation*

On Japanese Shopping Bags, Enigmatic:

London XYZ. All those floodlights spin your head around. Dance and prance across the stage shaking things in a peculiar way.

slogan on the side of a Japanese shopping bag

On Jesus Christ:

Why did He not marry? Could the answer be that Jesus was not by nature the marrying sort?

Hugh Monetfiore, British Anglican clergyman (later bishop), at a conference

On Jesus and Economic Theory, the Definitive Word on:

By no stretch of the imagination would Jesus have been a socialist.

Norman Vincent Peale, speaking at the Union League Club

On Job Qualifications:

A review of your application indicates that you are not qualified because . . . you were not selected.

EEOC personnel memo, 1973

On the Job of Secretary of the Interior, Cogent Observations:

We have to take care of those things—the land, all those things.

Manuel Lugan, secretary of the Interior

On Jobs, Fun:

If we're involved in a small war, we'd just go on with an extension of the present (mortuary) system. If we had 1 million dead, it would be more of a dump-truck operation. When I got this job, my predecessor told me, "They'll try to shove off planning for sanitary disposal of the dead on you. Tell'em we'll just dig trenches with bulldozers." We'll bury them, but afterwards we won't be able to say exactly what happened to Aunt Susie.

Harold Gracey, health service emergency coordinator

On Jokes, Dubious:

Since you're going to die anyway, you won't mind if we use you as a shield.

> *U.S. Customs agent David D'amato, to an art expert who was shortly going to be involved in a Miami sting operation to capture international art thieves*

On Jokes, Dubious:

He no play-a da game, he no make-a da rules.

> *Earl Butz, secretary of Agriculture under President Ford, on the Pope's attitude towards birth control*

On Journalism:

Journalists are not supposed to ask questions.

> *Singapore liaison for International Trade minister Datuk Seri Rafiday, at the airport, when confronted with journalists. (She quickly added "Except at press conferences," after seeing the incredulous looks of the journalist audience)*

On Judgment Calls, Bad:

Follow me around. I'm serious. If anybody wants to put a tail on me go ahead. They'd be very bored.

> *Gary Hart, presidential candidate who was forced out of the Democratic race when caught on film with a blonde woman on his lap*

On Judgment Calls, Bad:

Who would want to see a play about an unhappy traveling salesman? Too depressing.

> *Cheryl Crawford, Broadway producer of plays such as* Brigadoon, *turning down Elia Kazan's offer to produce* Death of a Salesman

On Judges, What to Look For in:

All I want is for my case to be heard in front of an impractical decision-maker.

> *Pete Rose, baseball player, accused of gambling*

On Jumping the Gun:

Let us see George Bush re-elected this November. And *then* we'll talk about 1994.

> *Vice President Dan Quayle, while campaigning for President George Bush, when asked if he was planning to run for president in the next election—which would be in 1996*

On Junkets:

This was not a junket in any sense of the word.

> *Senator Strom Thurmond (S.C.) who took his wife, two children, next-door neighbor, and eight staff members on a five-day trip to the Paris Air Show. Taxpayers footed the airfare bill.*

On Juries of One's Peers:

It was not my class of people. There was not a producer, a press agent, a director, an actor.

> *Zsa Zsa Gabor, talking about the jury that wound up convicting her of slapping a Beverly Hills police officer when he pulled her over on a traffic violation*

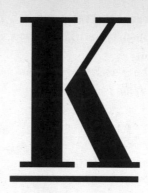

On Killing, Finality of:

Who he kills dies.

> *Jeffrey Archer, British politician and best-selling author of thrillers, talking about Saddam Hussein*

On Kinder, Gentler Thoughts, Presidential:

There are always going to be people who want to be President, and some days I'd like to give it to them.

> *President Bill Clinton*

On Kissing, Freud's Sexy Views on:

One special form of contact, which consists of mutual approximation of the mucous membranes of the lips in a kiss, has received a sexual value among the civilized nations, though the parts of the body do not belong to the sexual apparatus and merely form the entrance to the digestive tract.

Sigmund Freud, The Sexual Aberrations

On Knees, Where Found:

This amendment will put some starch in the backbones of weak-kneed college administrators.

congressman, during the 1960s, proposing to cut off financial aid to students participating in demonstrations

On Kuwait, Suggestions for Postwar Belt-Tightening in:

Instead [of having] four maids or three maids in the house, you can have two maids.

Abdel Rahman al-Awadi, Kuwaiti state minister for cabinet affairs

On Ladies, Definitions of:

This is no lady; this is a commissioner.

> *Escort of Federal Trade Commission Commissioner Elizabeth Dole,*
> *explaining to doorman, after she was barred from entering a male-only*
> *San Francisco club*

On Landlords, Where Found:

Ireland is overrun by absentee landlords.

> *Sir Boyle Roche, eighteenth century member of Parliament from Tralee,*
> *famed for his word mangling*

On Latin:

There are so many Latin players, we're going to have to get a Latin instuctor up here!

Phil Rizzuto, New York Yankees sportscaster

On Latin America:

The US has a vital interest in that area of the country.

Vice President Dan Quayle

On the Law, Experts of:

Don't just ask me about what's wrong with our legal system. Check with the opinion of that famous enforcer of American justice. I'm not talking about Oliver Wendell Holmes or John Marshall. I mean someone even more famous than that, Hulk Hogan.

President George Bush, during the 1992 presidential campaign

On Law 'n' Order, Maryland Style:

You need to stop and think before you get mad again. If you ever do it again, I'll shoot you.

Judge Perry G. Bowen, Calvert County Circuit Court judge, to a defendant convicted of disorderly conduct

On Laws, Interesting:

It is the inalienable right of the citizen to get drunk.

decision handed down in the case of St. Joseph vs. Harris, 59 Mo. App. 122 (Missouri)

On Lawyers, Moldy:

[He's] still green behind the ears.

> *Congressman Elford A. Cederberg of Michigan, referring to a young attorney*

On Lawyers, Similarity to Staircases:

I don't want to get into that, but Mike's got a whole new set of banisters.

> *Don King, boxing promoter, when asked if Mike Tyson was getting new lawyers to replace Vincent Fuller*

On Leadership:

People that are really very weird can get into sensitive positions and have a tremendous impact on history.

> *Vice President Dan Quayle, talking about current events*

On Leaks, Preventing:

To stop drip, turn cock to right.

> *sign in a Tokyo, Japan, men's room*

On Legal Defenses, Great:

I meant to kill my wife, but I forgot my glasses.

> *accused murderer of a passerby, reported in* Seattle Post-Intelligencer

On Legislation, Clear:

Notwithstanding any other provision of law, no trade benefit shall be extended to any country by reason of the extension of any trade benefit to another country under a trade agreement entered into under paragraph (1) with other such country.

part of the Trade Bill in the Senate, Section 4602

On Legislation, Groundbreaking Moments in State:

Any cook of either sex, white or black, of any and all nationalities and religious affiliations, hereafter shall make and bake biscuits of a size not less than six inches in circumference, to weigh not more than one ounce when done, always to be served hot.

Oklahoma State Legislature bill, introduced by Senator Fletcher M. Johnson, 1926–7

On Legs:

Reporter: Which leg did Paul Warfield hurt?
Don Shula (Miami Dolphins coach): I don't know. It's one of the two.

Don Shula, answering questions about which leg receiver Paul Warfield hurt during practice before the upcoming Super Bowl VIII game

On Legs, Where Found:

From the waist down, Earl Campbell has the biggest legs I've ever seen on a running back.

John Madden, CBS sportscaster

On Lesbians:

movie mogul Samuel Goldwyn, debating whether to buy Lillian Hellman's play The Children's Hour: Maybe we should buy it?

Merritt Hulburd: Forget it, Mr. Goldwyn. It's about lesbians.

Goldwyn: Don't worry about that. We'll make them Americans.

On Lies:

We lie by not telling you things. . . . We don't lie by telling you things that aren't true.

> *unnamed U.S. official, quoted in* Newsday, *January 11, 1991*

On Lies, Oliver North's Definition of:

[I] was provided with additional input that was radically different from the truth. I assisted in furthering that version.

> *Lieutenant Colonel turned politician Oliver North, discussing his role in the Iran-Contra affair*

On Life:

You don't realize what life's all about until you have found yourself lying on the brink of a great abscess.

> *movie mogul Samuel Goldwyn*

On Life, National Importance of:

Life is very important to Americans.

> *Senator Bob Dole (R-Kansas), when asked if American lives were more important than foreign lives*

On Life, Replaceability of:

The loss of life will be irreplaceable.

> *Vice President Dan Quayle, in a CNN interview, speaking about the San Francisco earthquake*

On Life After Death:

French railway president quits after second fatal accident.

> *from the Toronto* Globe and Mail

On Lights:

One effect of the better lighting is the improved visibility.

> *British politician*

On Lineups, Baseball:

I would be batting the big feller if they wasn't ready with that other one, but a left hander would be the thing if they wouldn't have knowed it already because there is more things involved than could come up on the road, even after we been home for a long time.

> *Casey Stengel, baseball great*

On Listening:

Gentlemen, listen to me slowly!

> *movie mogul Samuel Goldwyn*

On Lobbying, Truth About:

There's no connection between their lobbying work and the money they contribute.

> *Rick Evans, chief of staff for Senator Dave Durenberger, when asked if there was any problem with lobbyists paying the senator's bills, as quoted in the* Washington Monthly

On Lobbying, More Truth About:

As far as lobbying is concerned, this is a perfectly valid activity that any organization, scientific or business or otherwise, engages in. Most of our lobbying—in fact, I would say 100 per cent of our lobbying—is done for the benefit of the American people, and we're not ashamed of it.

> *Dr. Richard E. Palmer, president of the AMA during the 1970s*

On Logic, Bill Clinton's:

I've been criticized for doing more than one thing at once. . . . Would it be nice if you could pay your bills and not earn any money to them? I don't understand this whole—you can't do one thing at once. But anyway, that's what they say.

> *President Bill Clinton, at an appearance at a Cleveland shopping mall*

On Logic, Great Moments in:

This planet is our home. If we destroy the planet, we've destroyed our home, so it is fundamentally important.

> *H. Ross Perot, presidential candidate*

On Logic, Impeccable:

People say I'm extravagant because I want to be surrounded by beauty. But tell me, who wants to be surrounded by garbage?

Imelda Marcos, former Philippine first lady

On Logic, Irrefutable:

The first black president will be a politician who is black.

L. Douglas Wilder, governor of Virginia

On Logic, Nazi:

Upon being told that Hitler was dead:
I wouldn't believe Hitler was dead, even if he told me so himself.

Central Bank governor, Nazi Germany

On Logic, Sports:

Football players win football games.

Chuck Knox, football coach

On Loincloths, Gourmet:

Soaked for 15–30 minutes in hot water, strained and then added along with their soaking liquid, morels give a superb feral essence of loincloth to sauces and stews.

Leslie Forbes, writing about dried morels in Observer *magazine*

On Longevity:

There is not a man, woman or child present through whose mind the truth of what I have just stated has not been ringing for centuries.

Sir Boyle Roche, eighteenth century member of Parliament from Tralee, famed for his word mangling

On Losing:

You can pitch a gem and lose, but you can't lose when you win.

Eric Show, San Diego pitcher. A second later he added, "Wait, don't quote me on that. I sound like Yogi Berra."

On Losing Streaks, Inability to Explain:

It is beyond my apprehension.

Danny Ozark, Philadelphia Phillies manager, explaining his team's three-game losing streak

On Lost & Found:

A little boy has been found lost.

Tex Rikards, public address announcer at Ebbets Field, Brooklyn

On Love Letters, How Not to Write:

My dear Hortense . . .

. . . Farewell, my dear Adele!

Voltaire, famous French philosopher on an off-day

On Low Salaries, Why Certain People Keep Getting:

They are used to low incomes and to managing financial hardships.

Thomas Bull, director of personnel at Notre Dame University, on why not to be concerned about low salaries of university staff

On Low Salaries, the Little-Known Benefits of:

What if you are underpaid? Know the joy of being worth more than you get—the pure joy of unrecognized superiority.

Pittsburgh Reverend S. M. Smith

On Loyalty, Blind:

I have no idea what White House statement was issued, but I stand behind it 100 percent.

Richard Darman, budget director in the Bush administration

On Machines, Tasty:
Taste the difference among special machines.
CARBOY 1992, Japanese car magazine

On Madonna, Suspiciously Scholarly Leanings of:
[In watching Madonna's "Open Your Heart" video] we can't help but notice suspiciously academic references to Lacan's essays about "the

Gaze," Deluez and Guattari's "Anti-Oedipus," the feminist critique of woman's film image, and other citations too scholarly to be believed but too precise to be missed.

> *Eric Michaels, quoted in* The Madonna Connection: Representational Politics, Subcultural Identities and Cultural Theory *edited by Cathy Schwichtenburg as quoted in the* New York Times

On Madonna, Psychopolitical Leanings of:

The politics of sex and gender representations as they relate to identity has not been lost on Madonna.

> *Eric Michaels, quoted in* The Madonna Connection: Representational Politics, Subcultural Identities and Cultural Theory *edited by Cathy Schwichtenburg*

On Magazines, Targeted:

Mr. Bike: Magazine for windy people
> *Japanese magazine*

On Mail:

PS: If you do not receive this, of course it must have miscarried; therefore I beg you write and let me know.

> *Sir Boyle Roche, eighteenth century member of Parliament from Tralee, famed for his word mangling*

On Mailmen and Missiles, Similarities Between:

Neither snow nor rain, no, nor leaves nor gloom of night stays cruise missiles from the swift completion of their appointed rounds.

McDonnell Douglas Corp. ads, 1982, for the "missile of all seasons"

On Management Computer Professionals, Superstar Status of:

[Our speaker] has been described as having the stage presence of Mick Jagger, facilitation skills of Phil Donahue, and the inspirational message of Norman Vincent Peale.

Press release from the Society for Management of Professional Computing, Inc., as mentioned in Computerworld

On Management, Cozy:

I'll be right there and then we'll get into a cuddle.

Samuel Goldwyn, movie mogul, yelling to George and Ira Gershwin and George Balanchine, who had come for a story conference

On Man's Best Friend:

It has been said by some cynic, maybe it was a former president, "If you want a friend in Washington, get a dog." Well, we took them literally—that advice, as you know. But I didn't need that because I have Barbara Bush.

President George Bush

On Marriage, Great Reasons for:

Look at the f—ing world around us. It's an AIDS-infested world. And this woman is beautiful, talented, terrific, wanted by lots of guys . . .

Donald Trump, on his decision to marry Marla Maples

On Marriage, Worries of:

It was always a delight to be in Pali's company. "Life is too short to be grim always," Pali used to say mockingly, but never quite getting the approval of his charming wife who was always worried about her husband's filament.

obituary in India's Sunday Observer, *on cricket star Kirpal Singh*

On Meetings:

Reporter: I understand you had an audience with the Pope.
Yogi Berra: No, but I saw him.

Yogi Berra, during an interview shortly after he had met with the Pope

On Memories:

Thank you for evoking memories, particularly of days gone by.

Mike Ingham, announcer on BBC-2 TV

On Men, Varieties of:

Immediately every man in the place, including women and children, ran out to meet them.

> *Sir Boyle Roche, eighteenth century member of Parliament from Tralee, famed for his word mangling*

On Metaphors, Great Political:

This bill, if passed, will derail the ship of state.

> *Stanley Steingut, then speaker of the New York Assembly*

On Metaphors, Great Political:

What is being scattered to the winds here is not just a drop in the bucket.

> *from New York City Council debates*

On Metaphors, Great Political:

No one wants to say the sky is falling, but in this instance, I am afraid the emperor has no clothes. Despite Herculean efforts by the Council and Council staff, we are still only dealing with the tip of the iceberg.

> *Councilman Charles Millard, New York City councilman, in the first paragraph of a four-page press release*

On Metaphors, Mixed:

I have to say that people should keep their powder dry and not get fixed in concrete on issues such as this.

> *John Spellman, former governor of Washington*

On Metaphors, Strange:

They are getting in the thin end of the wedge by a sort of side wind.
Sir Ellis Ashmead-Bartlett

On Military Intelligence, Great Moments in:

In reference A, the cover letter at Reference B is an error. The additions at Annex B to Reference B are already incorporated in Annex A to Reference B, and are those additional items per pack that will be required if the complete schedule at Annex A to Reference B are approved.
British Ministry of Defense publication

On Military Intelligence, Great Moments in:

The nuclear protestors' pathological fear of nuclear weapons is something that is difficult to comprehend; after all, everybody lives in the nuclear age.
Gerald P. Hanner, retired Air Force Colonel

On Missionaries, Bloodthirsty:

Poor soul—very sad; her late husband, you know, a very sad death—eaten by missionaries, poor soul.
Reverend William Spooner, Oxford academic, famed for his tongue-twisting malaprops, called "spoonerisms"

On Mistakes:

We'll do right if we capitalize on our mistakes.

Mickey Rivers, Texas Rangers outfielder

On Modeling, Intellectuality of:

People think modeling's mindless, that you just stand there and pose, but it doesn't have to be that way. I like to have a lot of input. I know how to wear a dress, whether it should be shot with me standing up or sitting. And I'm not scared to say what I think.

Linda Evangelista, supermodel, commenting on the rigors of her chosen profession

On Modern Medicine, Some Great Things Brought by:

If somebody has a bad heart, they can plug this jack in at night as they go to bed and it will monitor their heart throughout the night. And the next morning when they wake up dead—there'll be a record.

Mark S. Fowler, FCC chairman

On Mom, Apple Pie, and . . .

President George Bush often talks of 1,000 points of light. I'd like to think those points of light are coming from the glowing end of cigars, cigarettes, and pipes across the country, and symbolize the cornerstone of this nation—tobacco.

Ellis Milan, tobacco distributor, as quoted in the Seattle Post-Intelligencer

On Money Management:

I'm so naive about finances. Once when my mother mentioned an amount and I realized I didn't understand, she had to explain: "That's like three Mercedes." Then I understood.

Brooke Shields, actress.

On Money Management:

When discussing the advantages of carrying bills in a money clip and credit cards wrapped by a rubber band:

But what do you do with your driver's license?

Jim Coleman, former Assistant United States Attorney, partner of top Philadelphia law firm Ballard Spahr Andrews & Ingersoll, famed for his malaprops, as collected by his colleagues

On Morale Problems:

Morality at this time isn't a factor.

Danny Ozark, Philadelphia Phillies manager, explaining why the team wasn't having a morale problem since falling out of the running for the pennant

On the Movie Business:

I go to the movies every night. Why not? I've got to do something to take my mind off of business.

movie mogul Samuel Goldwyn

On Movie Dialogue, Great Moments in:

Space officer: Well, what did you decipher? . . . Let's have it!

Space technician: It's just three words.

Space officer: I didn't ask for a word count, just give me the message!

Space technician: We've checked and double-checked. It keeps coming up to the same thing. The message is—"MARS NEEDS WOMEN!"

dialogue from science fiction film Mars Needs Women

On Movie Lines, Great Moments in:

The dead look so terribly dead when they're dead.

from The Razor's Edge, *1946*

On Movie Philosophy, Great Moments in:

[The movie *Amazon*] takes places in the Amazon and what you realize is that this man has to make major choices, and he makes major mistakes instead of the right things, and through his mistakes he learns a lot of soulful things, and he actually corrects his inner life, which, of course, helps enhance his outer life, and through the whole process we learn about how sad it is that we have something called the Amazon forest and we're destroying it, and yet I say as an American-Canadian actress, it's sad what we're doing to [forests] in America.

Rae Dawn Chong, actress, as quoted in Spy

On the MRS Degree, the Ivy League and:

It would be preposterously naive to suggest that a B.A. can be made as attractive to girls as a marriage license.

Dr. Grayson Kirk, Columbia University president, 1967

On Museums, Great Thoughts About:

The National Museum of Photography, Film and Television is tremendously important, both in photography, television and film.

Sir Richard Attenborough, producer/director

On Music:

There's not enough sarcasm in the musical score.

movie mogul Samuel Goldwyn

On Musicals:

Gregory Ratoff, film director: This is the greatest musical yet I have directed. It is sensational.

Jack Henley, screenwriter: Then why do you want to know whether I have time to work on the script?

Ratoff: I want you to work on it because it stinks.

SPECIAL SECTION: The Stupidest Jargon Words and Definitions

For some reason, governments and bureaucrats and technicians don't like regular words, the words that are found in a normal Webster's dictionary. They like their *own* words, their own definitions. You need a new type of dictionary to figure out what they're saying.

For example, you could be sitting in a crowded movie theater which suddenly someone runs in, screaming:

Help! Rapid oxidation!

That's the pithy nuclear industry way of saying "Fire." But by the time you've figured that out, you could be out of luck.

Yet it's a perfect example of a newly minted, completely confusing phrase that replaces a perfectly decent old word.

So why do they bother? Sometimes new words and definitions can make the users sound smarter than they are. And jargon words often make you sound cool. They're the verbal equivalents of Ray•Bans.

But the basic reason jargon words are used is to *hide* something from the public. Usually this means that the bureaucrat in question blew it and doesn't want us to know about it. That's when a lot of stupid definitions and words crop up.

And once bureaucrats get used to coining new words and definitions, they simply can't stop.

Some of the Stupidest Jargon Words and Definitions

Involuntary conversion of a 727 — plane crash (airline company in its annual report)

BOLT — sex
(biology of living today) — (British Columbia legislator who proposed replacing the word "sex" with this acronym, since sex was embarrassing to children)

Temporary meadows	clear-cut forests (U.S. Forest Service proposed term)
Premature impact of an aircraft with terrain	airplane crash (FAA definition)
Rapid energetic dissassembly	nuclear power plant explosion (utility officials at Three Mile Island)
The cognitive-affective state characterized by intrusive and obsessive fantasizing concerning reciprocity of amorant feeling by the object of amorance	love (from the *First International Conference of Love and Attraction*)
Located profitable areas for the concentration of resources	Bombing (from a Pentagon booklet)
Ideogram illumination intensity adjustment potentiometer	dimmer switch (from a 1974 Fiat 124 Spyder owner's manual)
ash receivers, tobacco (desk type) (The specimen should break into a small number of irregular shaped pieces not greater in number than 35)	ash trays (from a federal agency specification report)

| Pedestrian facilities | sidewalk (Arizona state report) |
| Automotive dismantler and recycler | junkyard (Pennsylvania legislature term) |

Finally, two definitions that break the mold—by being jargon-free, yet somehow more bureacratic than ever. These are dictionary listings from a government-funded dictionary put out by the Columbus (Ohio) Coalition for the Homeless—and they say it all. . . .

> **Emergency shelter for families**: *an emergency shelter which shelters families*

> **Homelessness**: *the state or condition of being a homeless person*

On Names:

There's a mistake in the scoreboard. They're only showing his Christian names, Ismail Ibrahim.

> *David Coleman, BBC sports commentator, known for his on-air gaffes called "Colemanballs" in England, covering the 1992 Olympics*

On Nature, Great Thoughts About:

You can't just let nature run wild.

> *Walter Hickel, governor of Alaska, explaining why he wanted state officials to kill hundreds of wolves*

On Nature, Great Thoughts About:

Wilderness is like herpes. Once you get it, it's forever.
Joe Hinson, forest industry spokesman

On Navy Parties, Entertainment at:

Streaking. Mooning. Ballwalking. Leg Shaving. Belly/Naval Shots. Chicken Fights. Butt Biting.
Chapter headings from the official Pentagon report on sexual abuse and lewd behavior at the 1991 Tailhook Association Convention for Navy aviators

On Negotiating, Hard-Line:

Either you give me what I demand or I'll take what you're offering!
Joe Torre, St. Louis Cardinals, during salary negotiations

On Negotiating, Great Tactics in:

I wanted to have all my ducks in a row so if we did get into a posture we could pretty much slam dunk this thing and put it to bed.
Lee Cooke, Mayor of Austin, Texas, explaining the secret negotiations for a new city manager

On Negotiation, Hard-Line:

I am looking forward to talking with you balls to balls.
Soviet Foreign Minister Andrei Gromyko, in response to Secretary of State Dean Rusk's "We're eyeball to eyeball and I think the other fellow just blinked," referring to the Cuban missile crises

On New Jersey Hotels, Why You Must Stay Awake in:

. . . no hotel, restaurant . . . shall be used as a sleeping or dressing room by an employee or other persons.

New Jersey law, passed in 1929

On New Laws, Good Ideas for:

If what our missionaries tell us is true, and I do not doubt it, we would learn a valuable lesson in the execution of law from dark, benighted Africa. Over there the accused is held guilty until he proves his innocence. If he fails to prove he is not guilty there is only one penalty—his head is cut off, stuck on a long pole, hoisted in a public place, and remains there thirty days.

J. L. Williams, in the Baptist Record, *1928*

On Newspaper Corrections:

We apologize for the error in last week's paper in which we stated that Mr. Arnold Dogbody was a defective in the police force. This was a typographical error. We meant, of course, that Mr. Dogbody is a detective in the police farce.

correction in the Ely Standard *(UK)*

On Newspaper Corrections:

An item in Thursday's Nation Digest about the Massachusetts budget crisis made reference to new taxes that will help put Massachusetts "back in the African American." The item should have said "back in the black."

correction notice printed in the Fresno Bee *(CA)*

On Newspaper Corrections:

A story in yesterday's *Daily* reported that SPY magazine publisher Tom Phillips said his magazine consistently refers to Donald Trump as the "short-fingered Bulgarian." The term Phillips actually used was "short-fingered vulgarian." The misquotation was not intended as a slur against Bulgarians. The *Daily* regrets the error.

> *correction notice in the* Stanford Daily

On Newspaper Corrections:

In an article on Monday, it was stated that Stephen Reynolds is the wife of Bonnie Wheeler. Steve Wheeler is the wife of Bonnie Wheeler. We apologize for the error.

> *the* Harrisburg *(Illinois)* Daily Register

On Newspapers, Talking:

I've only heard what I read in the papers.

> *Frank Burns, Rutgers University football coach*

On News Stories, Must-Read:

Frozen Semen Talks.

> *headline from an Australian paper,* Action China, *on Chinese-Australian business, in this case an article on a visit by the Victorian Artificial Breeders Co-op*

On News Stories, Must-Read:

London, (AP). Misy J orld2 Iceland's Hofi Karlsdhair xiz to Gyekjavpl hn Fripbya wion a smil p mzssaage for Soviet Leader Mikhwil Gorsachee and Ul.S Pgzxident Gonald Rcngwn whom she hoces to meets.

"It's a pewceful vhagntrif. . . " she ywid.

from the Indonesian Times

On New York, a Great Place to Work:

If people here [New York City] were not getting killed on the job in homicides, we would have quite a low rate of fatalities.

Samuel Ehrenhalt, Labor Department official

On Oliver North, Lack of Ambition of:

I'd rather not be introduced as a former White House aide or a former lieutenant colonel, both of which I was, but as a husband of one and a father of four.

Oliver North, who, incidentally, wore his lieutenant colonel's uniform, at his congressional hearing

On Notices in the Mail, Frightening:

You are currently due to expire 11/86.

notice from the Credit Card Service Bureau

On Nuclear Attack and Football Teams:

Consider a firm whose principal assets consist of a professional football team valued, preattack, at about $15 million. Suppose that the players survived the attack and that all debts of the team were fully paid up. Any plan to levy, for example, a net-worth tax postattack must face up to the fact that this firm's relative net worth in real terms is certainly not going to be the same as preattack.

> *Henry Peskin, Office of Emergency Planning, official U.S. government office charged with nuclear preparedness*

On Nuclear Deterrence Theory, Ronald Reagan and:

I think we're going to have to start a civil defense program. I think—see they violated and we kept to the premise that McNamara, in the original getting together and what resulted in our doing away with our antiballistic missile system, at a time when we were ahead of them in technology on that.

> *President Ronald Reagan, as quoted in* With Enough Shovels: Reagan, Bush and Nuclear War *by Robert Scheer*

On Nuclear Power Plant Tourist Trips, Fun:

A walk through the Visitors Center provides you with a close look at the work being done in Unit 2. Cleanup . . . decontamination . . . waste handling . . . all are performed with the safety of the workers and the public foremost in mind. And, weather permitting, you're welcome to

have your picnic lunch at the tables behind the Center. Enjoy your stay
We're here to help you.

Brochure for tourists from Three Mile Island nuclear power plant

On Nuclear Radiation, Why Not to Worry About:

All you have to do [to protect yourself from radiation] is go down to the bottom of your swimming pool and hold your breath.

David Miller, Department of Energy spokesperson

On Nuclear Radiation, Why Not to Worry About:

Plutonium is one of God's creations.

Gregory Morgan, Hanford Christian Nuclear Fellowship. Hanford was the site of a giant U.S. plutonium facility.

On Nuclear Weapons, Other Things as Dangerous as:

There are also enough rocks on Earth to kill the world's population several times over.

Lieutenant General Daniel Graham, Defense Intelligence Agency, explaining why it's necessary to have more than enough nukes

On Objectivity, Journalistic:

Conservative: An individual or policy that opposes change . . .

Liberal: An individual or policy that favors change. . . . It can also imply tolerance and open-mindedness.

Election Kit for students put out by the Los Angeles Times

On Offense, Need for:

Except for three big plays, we played well enough to win, if we had been able to do anything on offense.

Bart Starr, head coach of the Green Bay Packers, explaining why the team lost

On Olympic Coverage, Great Moments in:

There he is, the fastest man in the world this year. Other men may have run faster this year, but he did it when it mattered.

> *David Coleman, BBC sports commentator, known for his on-air gaffes called "Colemanballs" in England, covering the 1992 Olympics*

On the Olympic Spirit:

The Olympic spirit is to go out and beat the other athletes of the world, not to live with them.

> *John Stockton, member of the U.S. Olympics basketball team, 1992, when asked if team members were violating the Olympic spirit by living in a hotel instead of in Olympic Village*

On a 1–0 Score:

The game was closer than the score indicated.

> *Dizzy Dean, baseball great, quoted by George Will in* Men at Work

On One of the 197 Reasons You Should Enthuse Over Baltimore:

Over 1,100,000 hogs are slaughtered in Baltimore and packed each year.

> *from a 1926 Baltimore Chamber of Commerce pamphlet,* 197 Reasons You Should Enthuse Over Baltimore

On $181,000 Cars, Affordability of:

People who perhaps haven't had a Bentley before may feel one is now in reach.

> *Ian McKay, marketing director for Bentley's new Brooklands automobile, bearing a cheaper-than-typical sticker price—only $181,000*

On One-Word Descriptions:

Up and down.

> *Vernon Maxwell, Houston Rockets player, when a reporter asked him for a one-word description of his playing that season*

On Opera:

After attending a performance of Tosca:
It was pretty good. Even the music was nice.
Yogi Berra

On Opinions, Honest:

Tell me, how did you love my picture?

> *attributed to movie mogul Samuel Goldwyn*

On Opinions, Strong:

I have opinions of my own—strong opinions—but I don't always agree with them.

> *President George Bush*

On Opinions, Strong:

Basically, [I'm] a dog person. I wouldn't want to offend my constituents who are cat people, and I should say that being, I hope, a sensitive person, that I have nothing against cats, and had cats when I was a boy, and if we didn't have two dogs might very well be interested in having a cat now.

> *Missouri Congressman James Talent, when asked by a reporter if he were a dog or a cat person as quoted in* Spy *magazine)*

On Order, Sequential:

And now the sequence of events in no particular order.

> *Dan Rather, CBS anchor, during a radio broadcast*

On Pain, Definitive Summation of:

The pain is very painful.

> *Player Ze Maria, from the Brazilian national soccer team, in a TV interview, as collected by Paulo Cesar Martin and the staff of the newspaper* Noticias Populares

On Paralysis, Rhetorical:

This is unparalyzed in the state's history.

> *Gib Lewis, speaker of the Texas House, quoted by Molly Ivins in the* New York Times Magazine

On Paralysis, Rhetorical:

This session has been hit by an avalanche of creeping paralysis.

> *Stanley Steingut, then speaker of the New York Assembly, discussing the slow start of an assembly session (as quoted by Molly Ivins in* Molly Ivins Can't Say That, Can She?

On Parking in New York, Ease of:

No Standing, 7 A.M.–7 P.M. except Sunday
6 Hour Parking, 8 A.M.–7 P.M. Sunday,
Night Regulation 7 P.M.–1 A.M. including Sunday
25 cents per 15 minutes
Quarters and NYCTA Tokens only

> *New York City parking sign quoted in* the Bergen Record

On Party Platforms:

Our election symbol is the cock . . . which stands triumphantly to eradicate pain, to bring joy and to give women their pride. . . . We are ready to serve you, do command us.

> *Jayalalith, leader of the AIADMK political party in southern India (Tamil Nadu state); this is from the party platform, published in English and Tamil.*

On the Past:

The only thing to prevent what's past is to put a stop to it before it happens.

> *attributed to Sir Boyle Roche, eighteenth century member of Parliament from Tralee, famed for his word mangling*

On Pentagon Accounting:

If limitations on the authorization or incurrence of obligations under the provisions of DoD Directive 7200.1 (reference (15)) (hereinafter termed obligation limitations) apply to subaccounts below a subclassification level otherwise required pursuant to the foregoing, the applicable subclassification level will be further subclassified to show the subaccounts at which the obligation limitations apply.

Department of Defense Accounting Guidance Handbook

On Pentagon Pumpkins:

Good consistency means that the canned pumpkin . . . after emptying from the container to a dry-flat surface . . . holds a high mound formation, and at the end of two minutes after emptying on such a surface the highest point of the mound is not less than 60 per cent of the height of the container.

Defense Department specifications for the procurement of canned pumpkin, paragraph 52.2747

On Pep Talks, Presidential:

This is still the greatest country in the world, if we just steel our wills and lose our minds.

President Bill Clinton

On Percentages:

If there's a 50 percent chance we'll have a repeat American League pennant winner, you gotta remember there's also a 75 percent chance we won't.

> *Yogi Berra*

On Percentages:

I threw about 90 percent fastballs and sliders, 50 percent fastballs, 50 percent sliders.

> *John Butcher, Texas Rangers pitcher. To be fair, he stopped and said,*
> *"Wait, I'm beginning to sound like Mickey Rivers."*

On Percussion Instruments:

Last Thursday, an alarm was given that a gang of rebels in full retreat from Drogheda were advancing under the French standard; but they had no colors, nor any drums except bagpipes.

> *Sir Boyle Roche, eighteenth century member of Parliament from Tralee,*
> *famed for his word mangling*

On Perfection:

We've got an absolutely perfect day here at Desert Sun Stadium and we're told it's going to be even more perfect tomorrow.

> *Jerry Coleman, San Diego Padres announcer*

On Perfection:

This is a perfect scenario. It is the first time in my life that I've seen a perfect scenario. There's absolutely nothing wrong with it. I want you to have a hundred copies made so I can distribute them to all the other writers so that everybody should see a really perfect script. And hurry, before I start rewriting it.

movie mogul Samuel Goldwyn

On Permanence:

It's permanent, for now.

Roberto Kelly, Cincinnati Reds outfielder, on switching his name from Roberto to Bobby

On Philadelphia, Last Word on:

The only thing I know about it is that it's in New Jersey.

Michael Cropuzwel, ex-Dutch national team player and catching prospect for the Phillies when asked what he thought about Philadelphia

On Photographers, Wholesome Habits of:

I always carry chains in the trunk of my car because you never know when you'll need them. You know, you go out in the streets in Paris and you might want to chain a model to a fence.

photographer Helmut Newton

On Pitching:

I found a delivery in my flaw.

Dan Quisenberry, Kansas City Royals relief pitcher, on why he had problems with pitching control

On Pitching:

When a fielder gets the pitcher into trouble, the pitcher has to pitch himself out of the slump he isn't in.

Casey Stengel, baseball great

On Plants:

Myrtles are so common there that they make birch brooms of them.

Sir Boyle Roche, eighteenth century MP from Tralee, famed for his word mangling, describing what he had seen in South Africa

On Poems, Great:

Dentologia: A Poem on the Diseases of the Teeth in Five Cantos.

poem by Solyman Brown, dentist, published in New York, 1840

On Poems, Great Quotable:

In the words of George Bernard Shaw—"Two roads diverged in a wood, and I—I took the one less traveled by."

Indiana governor Evan Bayh, in a speech calling for educational excellence, to the Education Commission of the States, and misattributing the famous Robert Frost poem

On Political Campaigns, Taking the High Road During:

Known all over Washington as a shameless extrovert . . . [Pepper was] reliably reported to practice nepotism with his sister-in-law and has a sister who was once a Thespian in Greenwich Village. Worst of all, it is an established fact that Mr. Pepper, before his marriage, practiced celibacy.

> *Florida Senator George Smathers, in a press release attacking his opponent, incumbent Claude Pepper, in the 1950 senatorial race*

On Political Housecleaning:

Let's do this in one foul sweep.

> *Billy Wayne Clayton, former speaker of the Texas House, reported by Molly Ivins in the* New York Times Magazine

On Political Self-Assessment:

I am the real prick they wanted to remove.

> *Indian Deputy Prime Minister Devi Lal, in the* Times of India, *which omitted "pin" in front of "prick"*

On Political Self-Assessment:

Frank O'Conner grows on you, like a cancer.

> *Frank O'Conner, New York Mayoral candidate, describing his appeal to the voting public*

On Political Speeches, Great:

What we need to do in this campaign is unleash a people power that is second to none and make people thing and realize that there is help.

So the church becomes an important leg of this stool and without it the stool is going to collapse. I want a strong leg ... and as we make that stool, it's got to stand up on its legs. And it's got to be able to take the seat of that stool and do what it should be and that is turn people on to how right it can be in the state of California.

> *Dianne Feinstein, running for governor of California, in a speech in Oakland*

On Political Stances, Controversial:
I strongly support the feeding of children.

> *President Gerald Ford, speaking about the School Lunch Bill*

On Politicians, Ethical Standards for:
To forcibly remove a politician from public office, one has to meet a much higher standard of dishonesty.

> *Santa Barbara attorney Michael Cooney, replying to people who wanted to oust a city councilman who had switched price tags on items he was going to buy in a store*

Pollution, Pithy Thoughts About During the Presidential Campaign:

You talk about the environment—take a look at the Arkansas River. And I'll have more to say about that in a minute. We've even seen some chickens along the way. Here's one back here. But I can't figure that out or maybe he's talking about the Arkansas River again where they're dumping that—I've got to be careful here—that fecal—some kind of bacteria into the river. Too much from the chicken.

President George Bush, talking about pollution in Clinton's home state

On Poodles:

Michael Curtiz, director, arranging a scene during Casablanca: Wery nice, but I vant a poodle.

Prop master: But you never asked for one. We don't have one!

Curtiz: Vell, get one.

Prop master: What color?

Curtiz: Dark, you idiot, we're shooting in color!

[a few minutes later, Curtiz is called out to see the large poodle]

Curtiz: Vat do I vant with this goddamn dog!

Prop-master: You said you wanted a poodle, Mr. Curtiz.

Curtiz: I vanted a poodle in the street! A poodle. A poodle of water!

On Positions, Unwavering Presidential:

My position has not changed. I am—uh—pro—pro—uh—pro-life.

President George Bush, expressing his strong views on abortion

On Positive Outlooks, Excessive:

[A study is authorized on the] economic values of acid rain . . . before excessive amounts of money [are] spent to solve a problem which is at present a much greater economic blessing than a harm to our environment.

a resolution passed by Republicans of Wadena County, Minnesota

On the Postal Service:

I should have answered your letter a fortnight ago, but I only received it this morning—indeed, hardly a mail arrives safe without being robbed.

Sir Boyle Roche, eighteenth century member of Parliament from Tralee, famed for his word mangling

On Posterity:

People should buy thousands of these and save them for their ancestors.

Pete Hamill, journalist and then New York Post *editor, on a strike issue of the* Post

On Prayers:

The Lord is a shoving leopard.

Rev. William Spooner, Oxford academic, famed for his tongue-twisting malaprops, called "spoonerisms," trying to say "The Lord is a loving shepherd"

On Preciousness:

. . . one of those great couples—how lucky they are—based on personal and professional admiration. They are both unique artists, with so much to offer. And Emma is magic as a cook. At dinner she did something to a chicken that was an honor to it. The chicken sacrificed its life, but then had the distinction of being cooked by Emma.

> *Christopher Reeve, actor, talking about actor/director Kenneth Branagh and his wife, Oscar-winning actress Emma Thompson*

On Predictions, Bad:

What, Sir? Would you make a ship sail against the wind and currents by lighting a bonfire under her deck? I pray you excuse me. I have no time to listen to such nonsense.

> *Napoleon to Robert Fulton, developer of the steamboat*

On Predictions, Great:

Everything that can be invented has been invented.

> *Charles H. Duell, U.S. Patent Office Director, telling President McKinley to abolish the office in 1899*

On Predictions, Pretty Bad:

I don't think you're going to see a great, great uproar in this country about the Republican committee trying to bug the Democratic headquarters.

> *President Richard Nixon, four days after the Watergate burglary*

On Prejudice:

Mr. Speaker, if I have any prejudice against the honorable member, it is in his favor.

> *Sir Boyle Roche, eighteenth century member of Parliament from Tralee, famed for his word mangling*

On Presidential Candidates, Foreign Policy Qualifications of:

I've read about foreign policy and studied—I know the number of continents.

> *George Wallace, campaigning in the 1968 presidential race*

On Presidents, Honesty About:

The evening will conclude with a toast to the incoming president in champagne kindly supplied by the outgoing president, drunk as usual at midnight.

> *brochure for a club's annual dinner*

On Press Conferences, Great Moments in:

I've talked to you on a number of occasions about the economic problems our nation faces, and I am prepared to tell you it's in a hell of a mess—we're not connected to the press room yet, are we?

> *President Ronald Reagan*

On Press Secretaries, Great Moments:

Until the principals had agreed that this that which they wanted to do, plus that it was agreed on by those involved, and then it was—present it to the president for decision.

Larry Speakes, White House press secretary

On Principles, Political:

If a politician can't find a job for a friend, he shouldn't be in office.

Charles Youngblood, drain commissioner of Wayne County, Michigan

On Problems:

Things started to snowplow.

Kevin Appier, Kansas City pitcher

On Problems, Getting to the Bottom of:

We've got to nip it in the butt.

Jets coach, quoted by Gerald Eskenazi in the New York Times

On Problems, Minor:

We have problems with their support of terrorism, but we share a common goal.

Secretary of State James Baker, on the U.S. alliance with Syria, quoted in the Times of London, *September 19, 1990*

On Products, Innovative:

Keep your Anus clean—Taisho Pharmaceutical Co. has—marketed a cleansing foam agent, "I like cleanliness." . . . The "I like clenliness" whose soft foam contains sterilising agent and shark liver elements, not only sterilises, but . . .

new product, from Diamond Industria, *Japanese magazine*

On Profiting from Bills, Why It's Okay:

I'd just make a little bit of money. I wouldn't make a whole lot.

Texas State Senator Bill Moor, defending himself against the charge that he would personally profit from a bill he was backing

On Promises:

If you can't give me your word of honor, will you give me your promise?

Samuel Goldwyn, to a writer

On Promises, Absolute:

Can I make the promise I won't support [new taxes]? Absolutely. But, you know, sometimes you run into new realities.

President George Bush, when asked about his position on raising taxes

On Pronouncements, Bold:

President Clinton's rise to the White House at this unprecedented point in history probably destines his presidency for either considerable success or serious disappointment, depending on the domestic and international policies adopted.

David B. Bostian, Jr., chief economist/investment strategies at Herzog Heine Geduld, May 4, 1993

On Propriety:

Ladies are requested not to have children at the bar.

Norway cocktail lounge, sign from an exhibit sponsored by the European Community's translation service on the worst translations

On Psychosomatic Pain:

How could it be mental? I don't have a college education.

Steve Farr, Kansas City Royals relief pitcher, when questioned about his shoulder pain and asked if the soreness was mental

On the Public, CIA View of:

The press says that the public has a right to know everything. That's a load of garbage.

George Lauder, CIA spokesman

On Public Relations, Great Moments in:

Imagine waking up to radio reports that "Schools and businesses have been closed because of frozen pizza." Sounds ridiculous, but if all the frozen pizza sold in the United States each year was spread across six states, those radio reports could be true.

opening paragraph of a press release from the National Frozen Pizza Institute, as quoted in AdWeek *magazine*

On Punishment, Cruel and Unusual:

I'd like to find the leaker and I'd like to see the leaker filed—fired. Filed would be all right.

> *President George Bush, when asked about the leak of the memo written by EPA head William Reilly that urged a cooperative position at the Rio environmental summit*

On Puzzles, Puzzling:

Correction: Today we carry the answer for Saturday's Crossword Puzzler. Answer for today's Puzzler, was already printed yesterday. Our readers will find the answer of yesterday's Puzzler tomorrow.

> *from the* Jakarta Post, *Indonesia*

On Queens:

Let us drink to the queer old dean.

> *Reverend William Spooner, Oxford academic, famed for his tongue-twisting malaprops, called "spoonerisms," meaning to propose a drink to the dear old queen*

On Queens, Bloodthirsty:

The Queen Elizabeth I Hunting Lodge in Epping Forest: It now stands mute, but if you stand still . . . can you hear the ghostly notes of an English hunting horn? Or the last swish of a Victorian petticoat? . . . Where in later years, too worn to ride, the Queen and her favourites waited for dear after dear to come within bolt range of their crossbows.

> *from the* Chingford Classified, *Great Britain*

On Questions, Deep:

Tell me, general, how dead is the Dead Sea?

President George Bush, on a visit to Jordan. His host, General Zayid bin Shakr, answered "Very dead, sir."

On Questions, Deep:

[The question] is too suppository.

Alexander Haig, refusing to answer a question at a Senate committee hearing

On Questions, Important:

They say you have to stop eating when he does. But what if he's having a snack and you're starving? Do you have to eat fast?

Charles Barkley, member of the U.S. Olympics basketball team, on being introduced to Prince Rainier of Monaco

On Questions that Clear the Air:

We've got to pause and ask ourselves: How much clean air do we need?

Lee Iacocca on Detroit's resistance to tougher auto emission standards

On Quickie Society Childbirth:

Svelte and chic in the manner of her "elders" Gloria Swanson and Marlene Dietrich, one Miami Beach matron beyond 45 is amazing and delighting her friends by having her first baby in five months!

Gwen Harrison in the Miami Herald, 1952

On Quotable Quotes:

It's like what Yogi said—What *did* Yogi say?

*George Bell, Chicago White Sox player, when asked about his team's
prospects*

On Ramifistations:

This legislation has far-reaching ramifistations.
Gib Lewis, speaker of the Texas House

On Ramifistations, Bad:

It could have bad ramifistations in the hilterlands.
Gib Lewis, speaker of the Texas House

On Reading Habits, Presidential:

I don't think he's read the report in detail. It's five and a half pages, double-spaced.
Press Secretary Larry Speakes, when asked if President Reagan had read a report on the Lebanon bombing

On Reality, Dan Quayle's Grasp of:

We should develop anti-satellite weapons because we could not have prevailed without them in *Red Storm Rising*.

Vice President Dan Quayle

On Reasons for Appearing in a Television Commercial for a Military Contractor:

I'm the former chairman of the Ethics Committee. I know what's ethical and what isn't, and there is nothing unethical about this.

Senator Ted Stevens (R-Alaska)

On Recessions, Democratic:

On behalf of all of you, I want to express my appreciation for this tremendously warm recession.

Ron Brown, Democratic National Committee chairman, at the 1992 Democratic Convention

On Recessions, Republican:

I don't want to run the risk of ruining what is a lovely recession.

President George Bush in a 1992 campaign speech in Ridgewood, New Jersey. He meant to say "reception."

On Records:

Congratulations on breaking my record. I always thought the record would stand until it was broken.

> *Yogi Berra, in a telegram sent to Johnny Bench, Reds catcher, after Bench broke Berra's home run record for catchers. (Note: in his book* Yogi: It Ain't Over, *Yogi says this was a publicity stunt.)*

On Refinement:

The inhabitants already had, before the arrival of the Europeans, a considerable education and a certain refinement in the social customs, but were addicted to cannibalism.

> *from the German* Konversationslexikon, *on natives of the Cocos Islands*

On Reinventing Government:

"The predicate here is greater openness," asserted a White House official who asked not to be identified.

> *from a* Washington Post *story about a Clinton administration proposal to declassify documents*

On Relatives:

Was it you or your brother who was killed in the war?

> *Rev. William Spooner, Oxford academic, famed for his tongue-twisting malaprops, called "spoonerisms," to an Oxford student after World War I*

On Religion and Sports:

There are nights when Jesus Christ couldn't guard me, and that's one of the best feelings in the world.

Larry Bird, Boston Celtics player

On Religion and Sports:

I found Christ. I had a revelation while I was watching "Monday Night Football."

Terry Bradshaw, in a March 1980 Playboy *interview*

On Religion and Sports:

I think Jesus would have been a great basketball player. He would have been one of the most tenacious guys out there. I think he'd really get in your face. Nothing dirty, but he'd play to win.

Mark Eaton, Utah Jazz center

On Religion and Television Talk Shows:

I think, "What are those things Christ would want me to do? Would Christ get on that plane and fly to New York and go on the 'Phil Donahue Show?'" I believe he would, so I go.

Richard Viguerie, fund-raiser/lobbyist

On Religion and Unions:

Jesus Christ would be a member of the carpenter's union if He were on earth now.

Reverend Clement G. Clarke, the First Congregational Church of Portland, Oregon

On Religious Acoustics:

Q: Will you tell us about trying to sing, "Hail, Hail, the Gang's All Here," when you were in the temple?

A: We were told that an inharmonious sound could not be uttered in the temple. We tried to sing "Hail, Hail, the Gang's All Here, " and no sound came forth. We then just said, "Hail, Hail, Hail," and the words rang out as though amplified a thousand times.

Swami Baird T. Spalding on his trip to India, in Mind Magazine

On Remarks, Impromptu:

I think today that a few remarks I might make, we go back to the relationship in this great nation with the people who was the foundation of America, the people they've paid such a price that we may enjoy the blessings of enjoyment that we have, has been spoken this morning.

Evan Mecham, former governor of Arizona

On Representing All the People:

Students don't vote. Do you expect me to come here and kiss your ass?

Georgia Senator Wyche Fowler, to student-aged volunteers who were campaigning for deficit reductions. Fowler denies the comment, but the volunteers say he made it.

On Republican National Committee, Great Thoughts of:

... when the local government becomes too close to the people it inevitably leads to corruption.

> *Republican National Committeeman Van H. Archer, Jr., on his opposition to elect city council members from residential districts in 1977*

On Restaurants, Enticing:

Mattie's Restaurant and Yogurt Palace
"An Alternative to Good Eating"
> *business card of a restaurant in Decatur, Texas*

On Restaurants, Enticing:

Stomach Care Snack Bar
> *restaurant in Ghana*

On Restaurants, Unusual:

Jom Indian Restaurant
Business Hours: Monday to Saturday and Pubic Holiday
OPEN ONLY FOR PRIVATE PARTS AND CATERING SERVICES
> *Sign at a Singapore restaurant*

On Ringo Starr:

Who is she?
> *Casey Weldon, starting quarterback for Florida State, when told he would have a seat next to Ringo Starr at the Grammy Awards*

On Road wins:

All of the Mets' road wins against Los Angeles this year have been at Dodger Stadium.

Ralph Kiner, New York Mets' broadcaster, on air

On Role Models, Marla Maples and:

I'm so excited to meet you. I've always modeled myself after Ginger.

Marla Maples, starlet and girlfriend of Donald Trump, when meeting actress Tina Louise, who played "Ginger" on Gilligan's Island

On the Roman Empire, Great Insights:

It's like the Roman Empire. Wasn't everybody running around just covered with syphilis? And then it was destroyed by the volcano.

Joan Collins, actress, in a 1984 Playboy *interview*

On Rome:

Rome wasn't burned in a day.

Abe Hirschfeld, New York businessman and would-be media tycoon

On Royalty, Great Thoughts of:

Life is not worth living unless you have a choice of all the gloriously unhygienic things which mankind—especially the French portion of it—has lovingly created.

Prince Charles

On Running:

Carl Lewis, what a good runner. . . . All his arms and elbows and knees running in the same direction.

a British radio commentator covering the Olympics

On Running, Fast:

And Oprah Winfrey, she averaged 10 miles a minute.

Roz Abrams, Channel 7 Eyewitness News, NYC August 16, 1993

On Running for the Presidency, Good Reasons for:

. . . because I really couldn't think of a good reason not to.

Jerry Brown (who also said: "A little vagueness goes a long way in this business")

On Salman Rushdie, Interesting Simultaneous Abilities of:

Salman Rushdie knew exactly what he was doing. . . . He was playing with fire, sailing close to the wind and sticking his neck out.

Toby Jessel, BBC commentator, discussing author Salman Rushdie, who received death threats from Muslim fundamentalists for writing The Satanic Verses

A menu in a restaurant serves a basic purpose—to tell you what food the restaurant is serving.

But few restaurants are content with just the basics. In an effort to make the mundane more appealing, or to justify outrageous prices, or simply to sound "classier," many menus go for high-caloric descriptions—excessively cute or ornate language (ostensibly) designed to tantalize the reader. On these menus, it's not seafood, it's "treasures from Neptune's garden." Chops are "nested on a bed of rice." A green salad is "tender young lettuces gently tossed with a tangy dressing."

But sometimes these descriptions go awry—especially when the menu is written in a language other than the native tongue of the writer. Travelers abroad are presented with bills of fare that don't tantalize as much as mystify. In fact, in these cases, even when the menu is trying to be straightforward, something just doesn't come across. And even the very basic becomes very . . . interesting.

Here, then, are the best examples of tasty dishes from the Food Court of Hell.

Cold shredded children and sea blubber in spicy sauce
served at a Wanchai, China, restaurant

Indonesian Nazi Goreng
served at At Village, Hong Kong restaurant, from its "Exotic flavours of the Orient" menu section

177

Muscles of Marines/Lobster Thermos
Prawn cock and tail
Cock in wine/Lioness cutlet
French Beas/French fried ships
> *served at a Cairo luxury hotel, circa 1940 (which helpfully adds: "If you are wishing to show your feelings, wait until you see the manageress")*

Garlic Coffee
Sole Bonne Femme (Fish Landlady Style)
Boiled Frogfish
Sweat from the Trolley
> *served at various European restaurants*

Dreaded veal cutlet with potatoes in cream
> *served at Shangri-la Restaurant, Shanghai, China*

Rainbow Troat, Fillet Streak, Popotoes, Chocolate Mouse
> *served on Ladies Night at the Police Training School, Hong Kong*

Roasted duck let loose
Beef rashers beaten up in the country peoples fashion
> *served at one of Poland's finer restaurats, as appearing in an exhibit sponsored by the European Community's translation service*

Aside Rice Ham Fish
Crumbled Eggs with Tomato
Goose Barnacles

Natural Fish Knife (piece)
Gordon Blu
Thigh Lambskin
Pineapple Wirsche
Special Ice from the House
Frost Pie
  served at a Spanish restaurant, Moraira, Costa Dorarad

Hot coke
  Japanese resort menu

Pork with fresh garbage
  Vietnamese restaurant menu

Green sand bottle
  Sumatra restaurant menu

Fried friendship
  Nepalese restaurant menu

Strawberry crap
  Japanese restaurant menu

Toes with butter and jam
  Balinese restaurant menu

Chapped liver
New York deli menu

All vegetables served in this restaurant are washed in water passed by
our head chef.
Tokyo hotel menu

Dogs and croissant petty brunch
Japanese bakery menu

French creeps
Los Angeles restaurant menu

Fried fishermen
Japanese menu

Cuban livers
Japanese menu

Butttered saucepans and fried hormones
Japanese menu

Teppan Yaki—Before Your Cooked Right Eyes
Japanese steak house menu

On Sadism, Obvious Early Signs of:

From his earliest youth, Roger Chartier showed a curious propensity toward sadism. At seventeen, while still under age, he enlisted in the army. After his discharge, he entered a theological seminary.

from the conservative French newspaper L'Ordre, *1940*

On Salads, Atomic:

Be sure to put some of those neutrons on it.

Mike Smith, Cincinnati Reds relief pitcher, to a waitress when ordering a salad

On Salaries:

We're overpaying him but he's worth it.
movie mogul Samuel Goldwyn

On Salaries:

The tragedy of the Labour Party is not that their aims aren't sincere. It's just that they have this absurd obsession that high earners are rich.
Andrew Lloyd Webber, English composer of musicals such as Cats *and* Les Miserables

On Salaries, Meaning of Seven-Figure:

This is about more than tactics, than the mechanics of arriving at monetary figures. It's about values and philosophies.
David Cone, Mets pitcher, who got a multimillion-dollar contract from the Mets

On Salaries, Trifling:

It's not a million dollar a year contract. We're talking about a really large sum of money.
Larry Bird, former Boston Celtics player

On Salesmanship:

Here lies Jane Smith,
Wife of Thomas Smith, Marble Cutter
This monument was erected by her
husband as a tribute to her memory
and a specimen of his work

Monuments of this same style are
two hundred and fifty dollars.

epitaph composed by a marble cutter

On SAT Scores, Actor Modesty Concerning:

Yeah, I scored eight hundred on the verbal part of the SATs and 779 on the math. Why does everybody talk about this? Who gives a shit?

James Woods, actor, quoted in the September 1989 issue of Smart *magazine*

On Satan, Cricket Skills and:

If Christ came to Sydney today, he would be on "the Hill" at cricket matches driving home the lessons of the game. One can imagine Christ reminding the crowd that Satan was the deadliest and most determined googly bowler of all time.

Reverend T. McVittie, moderator of the Sydney Presbyterian Church during the 1930s

On Scores:

Twelve for 23. . . . It doesn't take a genius to see that's under 50 percent.

Dick Vitale, sports announcer

On Scoring:

Anytime Detroit scores more than 100 points and holds the other team below 100 points, they almost always win.

Doug Collins, basketball commentator

On Scripts:

This is a terrific script. It just needs a complete rewrite.

Peter Bogdanovich, director, to screenwriter Alvin Sargent, upon reading a draft of Paper Moon

On Segues, Political:

When I go out there on the lawn and I think about those kids, picking up Easter eggs, I want to be able to think about them all being immunized.

President Bill Clinton, commenting on the White House Easter Egg Roll, and trying to get Republicans for blocking his proposed stimulus package, which included funding for child immunization

On Self-Knowledge:

What's a Yogi-ism?

Yogi Berra, when Phil Garner, Milwaukee Brewers manager, told him he had said a Yogi-ism

On Sequences, Numerical:

He has just moved up the field from 25th to 30th.

David Coleman, BBC sports commentator, known for his on-air gaffes called "Colemanballs" in England, covering the 1992 Olympics

On Scientific Experts, Infallibility of:

Radio has no future. . . . Heavier than air flying machines are impossible.

Lord Kelvin, preeminent scientist of his day, president of the Royal Society

On Screenwriters:

Here I am paying big money to you writers and what for? All you do is change the words.

movie mogul Samuel Goldwyn

On Seafood, Bored:

Seafood brought in by customers will not be entertained.

sign on restaurant, Langkawi, Malaysia

On Secretaries, Duties of:

Secretaries for openings in college administrative areas. Good typing, word processing helpful. Able to interfere with faculty, staff, and students.

ad in the Irondequoit, New York, Penfield Shopper, *quoted by Herb Caen in the* San Francisco Chronicle

On Secretaries of State, Sexy:

I thought that Le Duc Tho had discovered some hidden physical attraction for me. He couldn't keep his hands off me.

Henry Kissinger, former Secretary of State, talking about the Paris Peace Talks during the Vietnam War

On Self-Assessment:

The next time I send a dope, I'll go myself.

Michael Curtiz, film director, to an assistant who had returned with the wrong prop

On Sequels:

We won't make a sequel, but we may well make a second episode.

Jon Peters, producer, talking about the movie Batman

On Service, Final Words on:

I want to thank each and every one of you for having extinguished yourselves this session.

Gib Lewis, speaker of the Texas House

On Sewers:

If this scene isn't the greatest love scene ever put on film, the whole goddamned picture will go right up out of the sewer.

Samuel Goldwyn, on a love scene in the 1934 film The Wedding Night

On Sex, Artificial:

Laboratory reproduction is radically human compared to conception by ordinary heterosexual intercourse. It is willed, chosen, purposed and controlled, and surely these are among the traits that distinguish Homo Sapiens from others in the animal genus, from the primates down. Coital reproduction is, therefore, less human than laboratory reproduction.

Joseph Fletcher, scientist

On Sex, Necessity of Sexual Maturity for:

Sexual maturation is an important factor in readiness for certain social relationships.

The 38th Yearbook of the Society for the Study of Education (1939)

On Sex, Never-Ending:

13) Aliens coming to the United States to engage in any immortal sex act.

U.S. INS law, excluding certain illegal aliens, including the above, August 1987

On Sex Appeal:

Drug Store Body. Let's get the Good Shape and have a sexy body just like a pig.

slogan on a pair of Japanese overalls

On Shall, Government Meaning of:

The word "shall" in the statute requiring prosecution doesn't really mean "shall"; it means "may or may not."

U.S. Attorney Stanley Harris, on why the Justice Department was not charging former head of the Environmental Protection Agency Anne Burford with contempt of Congress

On Ship Captains You Can Trust:

I cannot imagine any condition which could cause this ship to founder. I cannot conceive of any vital disaster happening to the vessel. Modern shipbuilding has gone beyond that.

E. I. Smith, captain of the Titanic *in 1912*

On Signs, Understandable:

No entry except for access.

sign in London, Victoria Street

On Signs, Understandable:

Parking for Drive-Through Customers Only

sign in a parking lot at a fast food restaurant, quoted by Herb Caen in the San Francisco Chronicle

On Silence, Sounds of:

Didn't you hear me keeping still?

movie mogul Samuel Goldwyn

On Similes, Explosive:

There are certain characteristics that come with the position and Joe Kelly just has the instincts of a fine inside linebacker. It's like being shot at in an airport with all those guys running around throwing hand grenades. Certain people function better with hand grenades coming from all sides than other people do when the hand grenades are only coming from inside out.

Dick Selcer, Cincinnati Bengals coach

On the Six Wives of Henry the Eighth:

As Henry VIII said to each of his three wives, "I won't keep you long."

President Ronald Reagan, in a speech in Moscow

On Size:

Gonzales is big for his size.

Howard Cosell, sportscaster

On Skin Diseases, Intoxicating Facts About:

Drinking is the cause of psoriasis.

Donna Shalala, Secretary of Health and Human Services, in a March 1993 speech—and meaning to mention cirrhosis, the liver disease, instead of the heartbreak of psoriasis

On Sleeping Habits, Odd:

I got a phone call from Jack Warner at one in the morning. He pulled me out of bed. It's a lucky thing I was playing gin rummy.

Michael Curtiz, director

On Slogans, Catchy:

The Southeast Asian Games is the Arena in Manuring the Sense of Solidarity Among the Nations of the Region.

banner in Jakarta, Indonesia

On Slogans for Airlines, Confidence-Building:

Air Vietnam: The most experimental airline.

slogan in 1960, (note: the French for "experienced" is expérimenté.)

On Slums:

movie mogul Samuel Goldwyn (on a movie set of a slum): Why is everything so dirty here?

Director: Because it's supposed to be a slum area.

Sam Goldwyn: Well, this slum cost a lot of money. It should look better than an ordinary slum.

On Slumps:

We're not exactly hitting the ball off the cover.

Yogi Berra, then Mets coach, explaining the problem with the Mets' hitting

On Slumps:

I wasn't in a slump. I just wasn't getting any hits.

Dave Henderson, Oakland A's player, when he finally ended an 0-for-20 batting record, April 1990

On Social Security, Great Administrative Moments in:

[Your benefits have been denied because of your death.] If you believe this information is not correct, please contact Social Security.

Official letter from Medicare, denying benefits to a retired housekeeper, (Kiplinger's, Personal Finance, *March 1993*)

On Socialites, Truth About:

We have this terrible image that we play all the time. I went to three balls last week and all of them were for charity.

Rose Sachs, socialite from Palm Beach

On Soft Drink Labels, Odd:

Good morning, dear lemons. How juicy you look today.

label on a Japanese lemon soft drink

On Song Titles, Hard to Understand:

I didn't know "Onward Christian Soldiers" was a Christian song.

A. M. "Aggie" Pate, event chairman for the Mayor's Prayer Breakfast in Fort Worth, Texas, when a Jewish leader complained that the nondenominational event featured the song

On Soviet Art, Why Not to Get Involved in:

You are welcome to visit the cemetery where famous Russian and Soviet composers, artists, and writers are buried daily except Thursday.

a sign in a Moscow hotel, referring to the graveyard in a nearby famous Russian Orthodox monastery

On Soviet Art, Further Reasons Why Not to Get Involved in:

There will be a Moscow Exhibition of Arts by 15,000 Soviet Republic painters and sculptors. These were executed over the past two years.

from an item in the Soviet Weekly

On the Soviet Union, Fond Memories of:

Gaiety is the most outstanding feature in the Soviet Union.

Joseph Stalin

On the Soviet Union, Sports Role in the Collapse:

They're running away from communism toward our way of life because of television and basketball. You play basketball in this country for a month, you go back, you're never going to be happy waiting in line for a potato.

New York Governor Mario Cuomo, commenting on the collapse of the Soviet Union

On Space, Way Out Thoughts About:

Space is almost infinite. As a matter of fact, we think it is infinite.

Vice President Dan Quayle, in remarks made while he was head of the Space Council

On Speeches, Stirring-Wise:

My goal is an America where something or anything that is done to or for anyone is done neither because of nor in spite of any difference between them, racially, religiously, or ethnic-origin-wise.

President Ronald Reagan

On Speechlessness:

I have nothing to say. And I'll only say it once.

Toronto Maple Leaf coach Floyd Smith at a press conference

On Spelling:

This ain't the way to spell my name.

> *widely attributed to Yogi Berra, when given a check saying "Pay to Bearer"*

On Spelling, Congressional:

Tudors Needed.

> *Representative Jim Bacchus, (D- Florida), in a letter to other representa-*
> *tives "looking for volunteers to tutor high school students"*

On Spelling, Improving:

Smith Corona: Introducing The Spell-Right III™ Electronic Dicitionary
This is the typewriter that catches a spelling error, erases it—even helps you spell it.

> *from an ad in Hong Kong's* South China Morning Post

On Spelling vs. Punctuation, Relative Importance of:

The *Rapid City Journal* and it's staff believe spelling is a very important skill.

> *letter from the* Rapid City *(South Dakota)* Journal *to members of an*
> *upcoming spelling bee*

On Spelling, Vice Presidential:

That's fine phonetically, but you're missing just a little bit.

> *Vice President Dan Quayle, to William Figueroa, Trenton, New Jersey,*
> *sixth-grader, upon seeing the boy's (correct) spelling of the word "potato,"*
> *which Quayle thought needed an "e" at the end*

On Spins, Communistic:

I don't believe the doctrine has collapsed; on the contrary, the collapse [of the European Communist bloc] proves that the principles are right and they applied them wrongly.

> *Vu Huu Ngoan, deputy director of the Marxism-Leninism Institute, Hanoi, Vietnam*

On Spins, Municipal:

A layoff is not good news, but it does provide other businesses and industries wanting to expand or move here an exceptional work force to choose from.

> *David Rumberg, executive director of the Hattiesburg (Mississippi) Area Chamber of Commerce and the Forest County Development Foundation, in the* Hattiesburg American, *after a local company announced layoff plans*

On Sports:

He slud in safely.

> *Dizzy Dean, Hall of Fame pitcher turned St. Louis sports broadcaster, on air. He once explained that "Slud is something more than slid. It means sliding with great effort."*

On Sports:

It's not how good you can play when you play good. It's how good you play when you play bad and we can play as bad as anyone in the country.

> *Hugh Durham, Georgia basketball coach*

On Sports:

That was a maximization of a minimization of hits.

> *Mike Macfarlane, Kansas City Royals catcher, when his team beat the Oakland A's 3–1 with only one hit*

On Sports, Great Insights on:

All of his saves have come during relief appearances.

> *Ralph Kiner, sportscaster, discussing relief pitcher Steve Bedrosian*

On Sports, Great Insights on:

I thought we probably played this week like I thought maybe we could have played last week, and I didn't even think we could play that bad last week if we play like this.

> *Ted Marchibroda, Indianapolis Colts coach, when his team lost to the Seattle Seahawks after winning their previous preseason game*

On Sports, One's Saints Should Know About:

If St. Paul were living today, he would know Babe Ruth's batting average, and what yardage Red Grange gained, but he wouldn't know anything about boxing, wrestling, or horse racing.

> *Reverend Dr. W. E. Grate, editor of the* Epworth *(Pennsylvania)* Herald, *in a 1926 speech to the 58th Central Pennsylvania Conference of the Methodist Church (as quoted in the* Williamsport Gazette-Bulletin*)*

On Sports, Strange Moments in:

Well, Burkhart's in the red—not only did he play it safely, he played it dangerously.

David Coleman, BBC sports commentator, known for his on-air gaffes called "Colemanballs" in England, covering the 1992 Olympics

On Sports, Strange Moments in:

George Hendrick simply lost that sun-blown pop-up.

Jerry Coleman, San Diego Padres announcer, during on-air coverage

On Sports, Strange Moments in:

Grubb goes back . . . back. . . . He's under the warning track.

Jerry Coleman, San Diego Padres announcer

On Sports, Strange Moments in:

Larry Lintz steals second standing up. He slid, but he didn't have to.

Jerry Coleman, San Diego Padres announcer

On Sports, Strange Moments in:

The tying and winning runts are on second and third.

Dizzy Dean, baseball great, on air

On Sports Players, Similarity Between Press Secretaries and:

I've learned that there's a time when it's in the team's interest not to say anything and in some instances not saying anything is really saying a lot. A lot of people understand what not saying anything means, so, in effect, not saying anything is really saying a lot.

> *Bill Walton, Portland Trail Blazers center, on why he wasn't commenting on controversial issues to the press*

On Sportscasting:

He didn't make the games exciting enough when nothing was going on.

> *Charlie Finley, owner of the Oakland A's, explaining why he fired one of the team's broadcasters*

On Sportswriters, the Problem with:

Sometimes they write what I say and not what I mean.

> *Pedro Guerrero, St. Louis Cardinals, on sportswriters*

On Spies, Why to Be Lenient with:

I am very patriotic. I've only committed one crime in my life.

> *John Walker, convicted as a Soviet spy, in an interview with the FBI*

On Squid, Virility of:

A squid, as you know of course, has ten testicles.

> *Graham Kerr, the Galloping Gourmet, T.V. chef*

On the Stanford Student Council, Constitutional Importance of:

What we are proposing is not completely in line with the First Amendment. I'm not sure it should be. We at Stanford are trying to set a standard different from what society at large is trying to accomplish.

Stanford University Student Council member

On Stars:

She's got talent and personality. Give me two years, and I'll make her an overnight star.

Harry Cohn, Hollywood producer

On Stitchery, Creative:

Upon presenting this ad with a US $50 purchase. You will receive our complimentary gift package consisting of: 3 hand embroidered handkerchiefs, 2 hand embroidered guests towels and one embroidered hot roll.

an ad in the Curaçao Gazette

On Stock Ownership, Politicians and:

I don't see any kind of conflict of interest for anybody, unless they have a controlling interest—51 per cent of a bank or something.

Texas State Senator Chet Brooks, on why his bank stocks and bank
loans didn't create a conflict of interest on his voting on bank legislation

On Strategizing:

Now if you have a strategy you say to yourself, "Well, all right, I'm going to get this out, but I'm going to do it in such a way that I do it in a manner that is compatible, or at least not incompatible, with my general thrust." So what you try to build is the implementation of your strategy by these incremental little things.

Secretary of State George Shultz, in the Washington Post

On Straight Answers, Al Gore and:

The theories—the ideas she expressed about equality of results within legislative bodies and with—by outcome, by decisions made by legislative bodies, ideas related to proportional voting as a general remedy, not in particular cases where the circumstances make that a feasible idea. . . .

Vice President Al Gore, on ABC Nightline, asked about President Clinton's withdrawal of Lani Guinier's nomination to the EEOC

On Strengths:

Lillian's greatest strength is her strength.

David Coleman, BBC sportscaster, known for his on-air gaffes, called "Colemanballs" by fans

On Strength:

Strength is my biggest weakness.

Mark Snow, New Mexico basketball player

On Subtitles:

Cowboy actor in a classic Western: Gimme a shot of redeye.

French subtitle: Un Dubonnet, s'il vous plaît.

On Suburbs:

The opportunity to visit Mexico is one of California's greatest attractions. Mexico is an adjacent area, in the nature, may I say, of a suburb of Los Angeles.

Senator William Gibbs McAdoo, in the Congressional Record

On Success, Early Signs of:

In the second grade . . . I punched my music teacher because I didn't think he knew much about music. . . . I not proud of that, but it's clear . . . that . . . early on I had a tendency to stand up.

Donald Trump, real estate mogul

On Success, Great Observations About:

If we do not succeed, then we run the risk of failure.

Vice President Dan Quayle, in a speech to the Phoenix (Arizona) Republican Forum, March 1990

On Suits, All-Weather:

You can wear this suit twelve seasons a year.

Jim Coleman, former Assistant United States Attorney, partner of top Philadelphia law firm Ballard Spahr Andrews & Ingersoll, famed for his malaprops, as collected by his colleagues

On Summing Up:

Even though there may be some misguided critics of what we're trying to do, I think we're on the wrong path.

President Ronald Reagan

On Summitry:

We . . . [must] avoid the tendency . . . to rush to summitry for summitry's sake and to bring about euphoric expectations . . . and then to dash that euphoria against the rocks of ill-prepared summitry.

Alexander Haig, former Secretary of State

On Sundials, Medieval:

Samuel Goldwyn (during a trip to England, looking at an old sundial): How does it work?

Man: Watch the shadow moving across the progress of the sun.

Goldwyn: What will they think of next?

On Superstitions; Foolish:

This guy is really superstitious. He doesn't even like to light cigars when he's close to a gas station.

Radar, Brazilian soccer star in the 1960s, complaining about one of his teammates; as collected by Paulo Cesar Martin and the staff of the newspaper Noticias Populares

On Surgical Strikes, Boomeranging:

There is no such thing as a surgical strike. . . . A scalpel can turn into a club and then have a boomerang effect.

Jeremy Paxman, anchor on BBC-TV, covering the Gulf War, January 1991

On Syntax, Athletic:

Sin tax? What will those fellers in Washington think of next?

Dizzy Dean, baseball great turned announcer, in response to the charge that his language was ruining students' syntax. Apocryphal.

On Syntax, Presidential:

I'm working on funding it just as close to what I recommended during the campaign, about putting people first.

President Bill Clinton.

On Syntax, (Former) Presidential:

We didn't give a timetable, but we've encouraged in every way these and more. But I'm just asking that people look at them. I have not seem them—maybe it's my fault—one account on whatever media of these steps put together as a package. Haven't seen one. So I'd like to suggest to the Congress that are debating this to take a hard look at this and see whether it's progress, whether it adds up to anything or, as some of our critics would say, it's pure, you know, boiler plate.

former President George Bush

On the Superdome, Impressions of Playing in:

It was a little different. It was like playing inside.

Steve Webber, coach of the Georgia Bulldogs baseball team, after the team played in the Louisiana Superdome

On Talking:

You couldn't keep a conversation going. Everybody was talking too much.

Yogi Berra

On Taste, Military:

We won't approve ads showing weapons drawing blood. We don't think that's in good taste.

Al Fraser, Navy Air Systems Command, on how arms manufacturers must advertise, as quoted in the Los Angeles Times, *1983*

On Tax Deductions, the Bottom Line on:

3 pr. underwear—$6

President Bill Clinton's 1986 income tax return listing deductions on items donated to the Salvation Army

On Taxis, Comforting Signs in the Back Seat:

SAFETY FIRST: Please put on your seat belt
prepare for accident.

sign in a taxi

On Tea, Never-Ending:

The Thatcher household did not spend 24 hours a day discussing politics over the early morning tea.

Carol Thatcher, daughter of ex-Prime Minister Margaret Thatcher

On Teachers:

Quite frankly, teachers are the only profession that teaches our children.

Vice President Dan Quayle

On Teeth, Where Found:

What is the use of all these countries sending us aid, and then below the table kicking us in the teeth?

Thai government spokesman

On Television, Quality:

Okay, our focus: Are Babies Being Bred for Satanic Sacrifice? Controversial to say the least. Unbelievable to say the least. Disgusting to say the least. We'll be right back.

> *Geraldo Rivera, host of TV talk show* Geraldo!, *introducing a commercial break on his show, October 1988*

On Television Commentary, Great Moments in:

[She] demonstrates normal logic—something she will abandon before she is 18 and will never experience again. Women's logic is one of those contradictory terms, like military intelligence.

> *Flip Spiceland, CNN weatherman, describing his baby daughter. Afterward, Ted Turner, CNN owner, forbade his on-air newscasters from doing any more "free-standing commentaries."*

On $10,000 Speaking Fees, Why Senators *Must* Accept:

I accept honoraria. I do not like to do it. . . . We do have grandchildren to educate. . . . If it were not for their grandparents, one of these grandsons would not be graduating as a physics major this year. Another grandchild would not be entering as a freshman to college this year. It is important that this country graduate physics majors, majors in mathematics, chemistry and various other disciplines in order to keep this country ahead in technology, science and physics.

> *Senator Robert Byrd of West Virginia*

On Tendons, Inflamed and Gene:

Whenever you get an inflamed tendon, you've got a problem. Okay, here's the next pitch to Gene Tendon.

Jerry Coleman, San Diego Padres broadcaster

On Tennis:

It was the 73rd career Grand Prick title for McEnroe, who was ranked No. 1 in the world from 1981–1984.

from an article on tennis in the China Daily

On Testimony, Great:

I got a little concerned yesterday in the first three innings when I saw the three players I had gotten rid of, and I said when I lost nine what I am going to do and when I had a couple of my players I thought so great of that did not do so good up to the sixth inning I was more confused but I finally had to go and call on a young man from Baltimore that we don't own and the Yankees don't own him, and he is doing pretty good, and I would actually have to tell you that I think we are more the Greta Garbo type now from success. We are being hated, I mean from the ownership and all, we are being hated. Every sport that gets too great or one individual—but we made 27 cents and it pays to have a winner at home, why would you have a good winner in your own park if you were an owner. . . .

Casey Stengel, before a congressional hearing investigation on the need for baseball antitrust legislation (as quoted in the Congressional Record, *July 9, 1958). Following this answer, Mickey Mantle was asked his opinion on the topic—"My views are just about the same as Casey's," he answered.*

On Thoughts, Deep:

I haven't thought about it. I'm not capable of deep thinking.

> *Phil Simms, New York Giants quarterback, when he had been shifted to reserve status and was asked if not starting bothered him*

On Threats, Very Scary:

[The Libyan army] is capable of destroying America and breaking its nose.

> *Muammar Qaddafi, Libyan leader*

On Timing:

There've been times when they've had hits from time to time, but they weren't timely hits at the right time.

> *Gary Carter, ex-Mets catcher turned television sportscaster for the Florida Marlins*

On Toilet Habits:

Before you defecate make sure there is no latrine around.

> *sign in Annapurna region, Nepal*

On Tongue-Twisters, Federal:

[Call 911 and] say these words: "There has been a life-endangering emergency at the Department of Justice Exercise facility."

> *step one of a list of instructions posted in the Justice Department's Occupational Health and Physical Fitness Program Facility (i.e., gym)*

On Top Hits, Catchy North Korean:

Care Shown for a Company's Hot House.
The Song of the 10 point political program
Let's Sing This Glory of Having the Respected Leader.
North Korean songs, performed by the North Korean Army Ensemble

On Tough Times at Beverly Hills High:

Unlike the show, the majority of cars are not Porsches and Corvettes. There are lots of BMWs and Jeeps.

Beverly Hills High School student explaining why the high school on television show Beverly Hills 90210 *isn't like the actual Beverly Hills High*

On Toughness:

Keep a stiff upper chin.
movie mogul Samuel Goldwyn

On Tourism Brochures, Catchy Communist Vietnamese:

Situated in the monsoon tropical zone, though the year covered with luxuriant vegetations, the land of Dai La by the Red River is "printed the forms of sitting tiger and winding dragon . . . looking all over Vietnamese country, that's land of scenic beauty, an important metropolistes indeed for four directions to gatter and the first rank of city merined to be regarded as Capital forever" . . .

From a tourist brochure in the new Vietnam, reported in Far Eastern Economic Review

On Tourism Claims, Dubious:

Even if the people in Haiti don't eat, they smile.

Michael Ange Voltaire, Haitian tourism official

On Tourism Claims, Enticing:

Enjoy French odor in the South Pacific.

from a French airline and government of New Caledonia ad

On Tourists, Picky:

People will put up with a strike if it means their room is not made up. But business would dry up overnight if they see people being killed, cars burned, or bricks thrown through coach windows.

Riccardo Dell'Erba, South African tour operator

On Train Delays, Reason for:

The train on the platform in front is waiting for a driver stranded on the train behind.

excuse to British Rail passengers waiting in a stationary train, quoted in the Economist

On Translations, Bad:

You are nothing but old nuts!

General McAuliffe's famous retort "Nuts" to a German demand that he surrender as mistranslated in a French newspaper

On Trash, Where not to Put:

An automatic incident report will be written on anyone found with trash in their trash can.

Don Williams, prison unit manager

On Trash Removal, Long Island Railroad Police and Unauthorized:

Not the paper you're looking for? You're under arrest for unauthorized trash removal.

Long Island (New York) Railroad police officer to woman picking up a newspaper from a recycling bin

On Trash Removal, Part 2, Long Island Railroad Police and Unauthorized:

This is for her protection. This is done to protect [patrons] from any other debris that might be in [the trash cans], like broken glass.

James Longaro, LIRR spokesman

On Travel Moments, Memorable:

Far up the river your journey is through mostly primary forest with impenetrable, undergrowth, Giant Orchids, Mangrove flowers, huge-tress with puthon crapping for branches, tropical bulfrongs . . .

Kalimantan, Indonesia, travel agency brochure

On Traveling, Helpful Tips in:

Upon arrival at Kimpo and Kimhae Airport, please Wear your Clothes.

from a Korean steel mill invitation

On Tributes, Great:

Tonight we're honoring one of the all-time greats in baseball, Stan Musial. He's immoral.

> *Johnny Logan, former shortstop turned sportscaster, at an awards banquet in honor of Musial*

On Tributes, Great:

In eloquence of expression he had no peers and few equals.

> *President Richard Nixon in a eulogy of Adlai Stevenson*

On Tricky Technical Points, Bill Clinton's Mastery of:

They've managed to keep their unemployment low although their overall unemployment is high.

> *President Bill Clinton, discussing taxes and employment*

On Trios:

You guys make a fine pair.

> *Yogi Berra, while walking toward a group of three players, quoted by Alan Truex of the* Houston Chronicle *in* Baseball Digest, *June 1987*

On Trust, Communist:

Do not touch anything unnecessarily. Beware of pretty girls in dance halls and parks who may be spies, as well as bicycles, revolvers, uniforms, arms, dead horses, and men lying on roads—they are not there accidentally.

> *Soviet infantry manual, issued in the 1930s*

On Trust, Communist:

Foreign embassies, businessmen, students, and journalists all try to play the "friendship card." They chat, leave their addresses, invite you to parties to watch obscene films. . . . Then they pull you under the water and you tell national secrets to foreigners.

> *from the Chinese publication* Counter-Espionage: Protecting Secrets and National Security, *published by the National Defense University*

On Tuning Worlds:

Discover the tuning world you have never seen.

> CARBOY 1993, *Japanese car magazine*

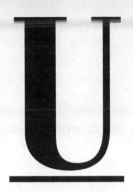

On UFO Abductees:

Many people are leery of fruitcakes in New York. When they find out you think you were abducted by aliens, they treat you like a weirdo, like you wear unmatched outfits or something.

> *Rosemary Osnato, UFO passenger, as quoted in the* Seattle Post-Intelligencer

On Ugly Sports Jackets, Trauma of:

In the end I said, "What's the matter? Is it the coat?" and I started to cry. . . . That was probably the worst day of my life, except for when my father died.

> *John Malkovich, actor, recalling a "kind of traumatic thing" that occurred when he was appearing in* Burn This *in New York*

On Undecideds:

It's no exaggeration to say the undecideds could go one way or another.

> *President George Bush, during the 1988 presidential campaign, discussing voters*

On Underwear, Proud Boasts About:

Sword underwear:
- Extra comfort
- More absorbent
- Extra strength
- Longer wear
- Meat resistant

> *label on Southeast Asian male underwear*

On Unemployment, Attractiveness of:

[We want to] make it less attractive to be unemployed.

> *Edwin Meese, Reagan Cabinet member, explaining that the Reagan Administration planned to tax unemployment benefits, Thanksgiving 1982*

On Unemployment, the Bright Side to:

We have more people employed in this country than ever before. Sure, unemployment is up, but more people are looking for work than ever before.

> *William Rusher, newspaper columnist*

On Universities, Great American:

He must think I went to the Massachusetts Constitution of Technology.

Dizzy Dean, baseball great, commenting on fellow player Branch Rickey's ornate way of speaking, quoted in Sporting News, *March 26, 1976*

On University of Georgia Athletics, Proud Boasts About:

We may not be able to make a university student [out of an athlete], but if we can teach him to read and write, maybe he can work at the post office rather than as a garbage man when he gets through with his athletic career.

Kevin Ross, University of Georgia attorney

On Unknowns, Known:

Samuel Goldwyn: We've got to get some new blood around here. I want to sign up a young writer, talented but completely unknown, who'll bring us new ideas and a fresh viewpoint.

Miriam Howell, Goldwyn's assistant: I know just the man for you . . . a young playwright by the name of John Patrick.

Goldwyn: Never heard of him. Who else can you come up with?

On Unknowns, Unknown:

In the John Hancock, there were unknown unknowns. In this case, we just have unknowns.

Chief Engineer John Carbone of the Government Center Commission, on glass panes falling from government buildings (not as many as fell from the John Hancock Building)

On Unmacho:

When I see these guys write all this macho stuff I want to smash their heads.

John Turturro, screenwriter

On Unpacking Boxes, Unusual Instructions:

1) Depend on installation schedule, depacking shall be done from necessary parts . . .

5) Packing of electricity shall be kept inside of factory as soon as possible.

from a Japanese shipment of machine tools

On Upbringing, Tough:

Our parents were of Midwestern stock and very strict. They didn't want us to grow up to be spoiled and rich. If we left our tennis rackets out in the rain, we were punished.

Nancy Ellis, sister of former president George Bush

On Upbringing, Tough:

People have this impression that we came from an upper-class upbringing because we had a Citroën and three kids went to a private school.

Joie Lee, Spike Lee's sister, answering accusations that her brother isn't the tough street-smart person he pretends to be

On Vacation Spots:

One of those Canadian proverbs.

Brewer's Jim Gantner, on being asked where he went on a hunting vacation

On Venezuela:

That's the Italian city with the guys in the boats, right?

Murad Muhammad, boxing promoter, after being told he might arrange a fight with another promoter in Venezuela

On Verbosity:

Verbosity leads to unclear, inarticulate things.

Vice President Dan Quayle

On Verbs, New:

We were not microgramming Grenada intelligencewise until about that time frame.

Admiral Wesley L. MacDonald, Navy spokesman

On Viewing Habits, Presidential:

I watch a lot of baseball on radio.

President Gerald Ford, on ABC-TV's Monday Night Baseball, *1978, as quoted in Bob Chieger's* Voices of Baseball

On Vision:

Some reporters said I don't have any vision. I don't see that.

President George Bush

On Voices:

Do not look at me in that tone of voice.

Senator Thaddeus Caraway (D-Arkansas), in a 1929 Congressional Record

On Volunteers, Army:

The only way we'll ever get a volunteer army is to draft them.

Chairman of the House Committee on Armed Services F. Edward Hebert. He was serious.

On Voting in Arkansas, Impossibility of:

And no person shall be permitted under any pretext whatever, to come nearer than fifty feet of any door or window of any polling room, from the opening of the polls until completion of the count and the certification of the returns.

Arkansas Law, section 4761, Pope's Digest

On Walking, Helpful Government Report of What Is:

Walking is here defined as a means of travel from an origin to a destination.

Arizona state report on the benefits of walking, as reported in the Phoenix Gazette

On War, Experiencing:

I don't like war. I have never been to a war, but I have seen "The Killing Fields."

Fawn Hall, assistant to Oliver North

On War, When It Isn't:

We are not at war with Egypt. We are in armed conflict.

Sir Anthony Eden, British Prime Minister, in 1956

On Warnings on Batman Costumes, Helpful:

Caution: Cape does not enable user to fly.

instructions on Kenner Products' Batman costume

On Watergate, Good Things About:

No, I'm not sorry. I'm glad I gave to Nixon. Watergate was good for the country. It allowed us to define standards of public morality.

W. Clement Stone, Chicago insurance executive, when asked if he regretted giving over $200,000 to Richard Nixon's campaign in 1968 and $2 million in 1972

On Watergate, Unimportance of:

I'd like to see people, instead of spending so much time on the ethical problem, get after the problems that really affect the people of this country.

President Richard Nixon

On Weaknesses:

Well, I'd say our greatest weakness is our lack of strength. Of course, I think you'll see some improvement as we get better.

a coach asked about his football team's prospects, as quoted in the Charleston (West Virginia) Gazette

On Weaknesses:

D. W. Griffith: You say you've never made a picture before?
movie mogul Samuel Goldwyn: Yes, but that is our strongest weak point.

On Weapons, Revolutionary Government Ideas About:

. . . human factors should be an important consideration . . . to be sure that weapons systems can be operated and maintained by the people who must use them.

U.S. General Accounting Office in a report

On Weather, Politically Correct Thoughts About:

Weather's like rape—long as it's inevitable, you might as well lie back and enjoy it.

Clayton Williams, Texas businessman and then Republican candidate for governor of Texas

On Weather Forecasting:

We are unable to announce the weather. We depend on weather reports from the airport, which is closed, due to the weather. Whether we will be able to give you the weather tomorrow will depend on the weather.

from the Arab News

On Well-Wishers:

. . . the health of Mr. Parnell has lately taken a very serious turn, and fears of his recovery are entertained by his friends.

From a Dublin newspaper, reprinted by Irish and English papers, 1890

On Lawrence Welk:

I'm all for Lawrence Welk. Lawrence Welk is a wonderful man. He used to be, or was, or—wherever he is now, bless him.

President George Bush, campaigning in the New Hampshire primary, in a speech about the line-item veto

On What Not to Say at a French Diplomatic Party:

Are you a dung-hill?

Englishwomen, asking for a light in French, and using the wrong word, recounted by Sir Robert Bruce Lockhart

On Whiskey, Unusual:

World finest whiskey made from Scotland's finest grapes.

advertisement for a Japanese whiskey

On Wind:

The wind at Candlestick tonight is blowing with great propensity.

Ron Fairly, San Francisco Giants broadcaster

On Winds, Communist:

It got up in the Sandanista winds.

Andy Van Slyke, St. Louis Cardinals outfielder, explaining why he couldn't catch a ball at Dodger Stadium—and trying to refer to California's famous Santa Ana winds

On Wines, Swiss:

Our wines leave you nothing to hope for.

Swiss restaurant, from an exhibit sponsored by the European Community's translation service

On Winning:

You wouldn't have won if we had beaten you.

Yogi Berra to Los Angeles Dodgers executive Al Campanis

On Winning:

As I say, if we score more goals than them, then we'll win.

Kenny Dalgleish, UK soccer player

On Winning:

The only reason we're 7–0 is because we've won all seven of our games.

Dave Garcia, interim Cleveland Indians manager, deftly explaining why the team had won the first seven games since he had taken over as manager

On Winning:

When you're not winning, it's tough to win a game.

> *Tony LaRussa, Oakland A's manager, explaining why the team's 1987 season had gotten off to a slow start*

On Wisdom, Senatorial:

Average voters don't have access to the knowledge needed for informed judgments.

> *Dan Evans, Washington State Senator*

On Women, Appreciation of:

In my young days, I used to pick up sluts, and I don't mean that nastily. It's more a term of endearment, really, for girls who know how to speak their minds.

> *actor Kevin Costner*

On Women, Appreciation of:

Why can't a woman be more like a dog, huh? So sweet, loving, attentive.

> *Kirk Douglas, quoted in* New Woman

On Women, Ballistic:

Weapons are a lot like women. Everyone wants one a little different.

> *Lu Hindery, sheriff, Alachua County, Florida, quoted in the* Gainesville Sun

On Women Journalists, Congressional Attitude Toward:

We're going to put you back in the fashion department.

> *Congressperson Fred Grandy, answering a question from a female reporter*

On Women Journalists, Dubious Summations of:

They're trying to prove their manhood.

> *H. Ross Perot, Texas billionaire and periodic political figure, then-presidential candidate, about the female reporters who asked him difficult questions*

On Women Journalists, Fun Jokes About:

They've both seen Patriot missiles up close.

> *Victor Kiam, owner of the Boston Patriots, giving the punch line to a joke about the similarities between Lisa Olsen, Boston sports reporter, and Saddam Hussein*

On Wrists:

She [Monica Seles] has so much control of the racket with those double-handed wrists.

> *Virginia Wade, ex-tennis star turned broadcaster, covering a tennis match on air*

On Writers:

How'm I gonna do decent pictures when all my good writers are in jail? . . . Don't misunderstand me, they all ought to be hung.

movie mogul Samuel Goldwyn, quoted by Dorothy Parker in Writers at Work: First Series, *1958*

On Youneverknow:

There is one word in America that says it all, and that one word is "You never know."

Joaquin Andujar, former Houston Astro pitcher

On Youth:

Youth lacks, to some extent, experience.

Vice President Spiro T. Agnew

On Youthful Appearances, How to Keep:

Well, I used to look like this when I was young and now I still do.

Yogi Berra, baseball great and then Mets coach, to a reporter who asked him how he kept looking so young, in Sporting News, *July 11, 1970*

On a 0–19 Loss Record:

I guess he didn't get off to such a good start.

> *Buddy Groom, Detroit Tigers rookie pitcher, after being told that the record for losses by a rookie pitcher was 0–19, set by the Washington Senators' Robert Groom in 1909*